Mnemonology

ESSAYS IN COGNITIVE PSYCHOLOGY

North American Editors:
Henry L. Roediger, III, *Washington University in St. Louis*
James R. Pomerantz, *Rice University*

European Editors:
Alan D. Baddeley, *University of York*
Vicki Bruce, *University of Edinburgh*
Jonathan Grainger, *Université de Provence*

Essays in Cognitive Psychology is designed to meet the need for rapid publication of brief volumes in cognitive psychology. Primary topics will include perception, movement and action, attention, memory, mental representation, language and problem solving. Furthermore, the series seeks to define cognitive psychology in its broadest sense, encompassing all topics either informed by, or informing, the study of mental processes. As such, it covers a wide range of subjects including computational approaches to cognition, cognitive neuroscience, social cognition, and cognitive development, as well as areas more traditionally defined as cognitive psychology. Each volume in the series will make a conceptual contribution to the topic by reviewing and synthesizing the existing research literature, by advancing theory in the area, or by some combination of these missions. The principal aim is that authors will provide an overview of their own highly successful research program in an area. It is also expected that volumes will, to some extent, include an assessment of current knowledge and identification of possible future trends in research. Each book will be a self-contained unit supplying the advanced reader with a well-structured review of the work described and evaluated.

Forthcoming

Mulligan: *Implicit Memory*
Brown: *Tip-of-the-tongue Phenomenon*
Lampinen, Neuschatz, & Cling: *Psychology of Eyewitness Identification*

Published

Worthen & Hunt: *Mnemonics for the 21st Century*
Surprenant & Neath: *Principles of Memory*
Kensinger: *Emotional Memory Across the Lifespan*
Millar: *Space and Sense*
Evans: *Hypothetical Thinking*
Gallo: *Associative Illusions of Memory*
Cowan: *Working Memory Capacity*
McNamara: *Semantic Priming*
Brown: *The Déjà Vu Experience*
Coventry & Garrod: *Saying, Seeing and Acting*
Robertson: *Space, Objects, Minds and Brains*
Cornoldi & Vecchi: *Visuo-spatial Working Memory and Individual Differences*
Sternberg, et al.: *The Creativity Conundrum*
Poletiek: *Hypothesis-testing Behaviour*
Garnham: *Mental Models and the Interpretations of Anaphora*
Evans & Over: *Rationality and Reasoning*
Engelkamp: *Memory for Actions*

For updated information about published and forthcoming titles in the *Essays in Cognitive Psychology* series, please visit: **www.psypress.com/essays**

Mnemonology

Mnemonics for the 21st Century

JAMES B. WORTHEN AND R. REED HUNT

Psychology Press
Taylor & Francis Group

New York London

Psychology Press
Taylor & Francis Group
270 Madison Avenue
New York, NY 10016

Psychology Press
Taylor & Francis Group
27 Church Road
Hove, East Sussex BN3 2FA

Printed in the United States of America on acid-free paper
10 9 8 7 6 5 4 3 2 1

International Standard Book Number: 978-1-84169-894-6 (Hardback)

Library of Congress Cataloging-in-Publication Data

Worthen, James B.
   Mnemonology : mnemonics for the 21st century / James B. Worthen, R. Reed Hunt.
       p. cm. -- (Essays in cognitive psychology)
       Includes bibliographical references and index.
       ISBN 978-1-84169-894-6 (hardcover : alk. paper)
       1. Mnemonics. I. Hunt, R. Reed. II. Title.

BF385.W77 2010
153.1′4--dc22   2010017124

Visit the Taylor & Francis Web site at
http://www.taylorandfrancis.com

and the Psychology Press Web site at
http://www.psypress.com

To my son B for all the fun and laughter he brings me each day.

—JBW

To Rebekah.

—RRH

CONTENTS

PREFACE

It is not uncommon for professors and teachers of psychology to approach the topic of mnemonics with uneasiness. Coverage of mnemonics in introductory psychology courses and some courses in cognitive psychology is often considered a somewhat outdated tradition. Moreover, even those who accept the merit of tradition tend to be skeptical about the overall utility of mnemonics and mnemonic instruction. Over the course of time, the definition of mnemonics has become narrow, and a lack of enthusiasm in the topic seems to have relegated this ancient art to the rank of a historical curiosity. As a result, mnemonics has been placed on the back burner of empirical psychology in the past two decades. It is our hope that this book revives interest in mnemonics by showing that the topic remains fertile for psychological researchers, educators, and students of psychology.

We are grateful to Roddy Roediger for suggesting this project and for advice on its development. Russell Carney read the entire manuscript and offered constructive comments that improved the final version, as did two other anonymous reviewers. Paul Dukes and Stephanie Drew at Psychology Press provided all of the support and encouragement an author could want. Their efforts were invaluable in seeing the book to completion.

Is There a Place for Mnemonics in Modern Psychology?

Mnemonics is a peculiar invention. No other artifact has been created for the sole purpose of supporting a natural psychological process that already is functioning perfectly in its natural form. The psychological process of course is memory.

The very existence of mnemonics is a testament to the central importance of memory for myriad human endeavors, but, in a subtle contradiction, the creation of mnemonics exposes a belief that the naturally evolved, bio/psychological process of memory is inadequate to accomplish many of these activities. To compensate for the perceived deficiency in the natural process, we invented an artifact: mnemonic techniques.

The development and use of mnemonic devices have a very long history. Over this time frame, many specific techniques have been devised, and in some subset of those, their effectiveness has been documented, more or less convincingly, as bona fide memory prostheses. Given that most people seem to believe that their memory is not as good as they would like for it to be, one might expect widespread education about and enthusiasm for mnemonics. Although there have been periods in history when such was the case, today is not one of them. Why not? This is a question that we shall pursue in this chapter as we briefly trace highlights of the history of mnemonics.

As we shall see, enthusiasm for mnemonics has been cyclical for centuries now. The formally devised systems can be elaborate and complex and have always been viewed as artificial. Sentiment concerning the use of mnemonics varies with the perceived relationship between the artificial techniques and natural memory. Although never clearly defined, natural memory was historically taken to be the natural processes of memory, sometimes described as God given, that operate without artifactual intervention (Yates, 1966). The positive view of mnemonics is of an art that created an assistant to the natural memory processes. The negative view is of a set of tricks that at best produces gimmickry and at worse interference with the natural processes. At the end of the historical account in this chapter, we shall directly confront this tension and propose a modern reconciliation that will bring the art of memory into the mainstream of memory science.

☐ First Records of Mnemonic Use

As long as humans have inhabited the earth, it is likely that there has been reliance on and attempts to improve memory. Early hunter-gatherer societies would have used memory to know where game and other forage could be located at different times of year, and, in fact, archaeological evidence suggests that external mnemonics were first used 28,000 years ago (D'Errico, 2001). External mnemonics are cues placed in the environment in order to improve memory. Modern examples of external mnemonics include writing a reminder on paper or circling a date on a calendar. Evidence suggests that during the Upper Paleolithic period, primitive humans marked wood and bones with notches to keep cumulative records of cyclical events (Wynn & Coolidge, 2003). Although the specific events being recorded are not known, it is not difficult to accept the possibility that these primitive mnemonics were used much like a modern hunter might refer to a calendar or solunar tables to determine where and when to locate wild game. For example, primitive hunters may have charted cycles of animal migration and used the records as reminders of where to locate seasonal food sources. In any event, it is interesting to note that these primitive external mnemonics are believed to have served the same functions that modern-day external mnemonics serve: to reduce working-memory load and to minimize dependence on long-term storage and retrieval (Wynn & Coolidge, 2003). Modern use of external mnemonics will be discussed in Chapter 2.

☐ Internal Mnemonics and Oral Culture

An internal mnemonic is a cognitive strategy designed to enhance the encoding (initial processing) of information. If a mnemonic successfully enhances encoding, then, in theory, it should also facilitate the storage and retrieval of the information. As such, one might view an internal mnemonic as a strategy that serves to prepare to-be-remembered information such that it can be properly filed away in memory and thus easily accessed when needed.

The evolution of psychosocial processes, especially language and communication, required memory for detail that biological evolution had not (de Chardin, 1959). The demands that early oral traditions placed on reproductive memory are well documented (e.g., Rubin, 1995; Yates, 1966), and because natural memory had not evolved for such purposes, artificial support for the natural processes was required to develop and maintain oral genres. In the absence of widespread literacy, external mnemonics would have been unavailable for the new demands on memory. Development of cognitive strategies to support such memory constitutes an important psychological adaptation to meet the new sociocultural demands.

As documented below, the use of internal mnemonics indeed was ubiquitous in ancient cultures with strong oral traditions. In fact, at least one major theory of orality (Ong, 2002) includes the use of mnemonics as one of the defining characteristics of oral culture. Among the internal mnemonics used by ancient orators, visual mental imagery was a dominant theme.

An example of the early use of an imagery-based mnemonic is found in Marcus Tullius Cicero's *De Oratore*, which was written in 55 BC (Yates, 1966). In *De Oratore*, Cicero conveys the story of Simonides of Ceos (556 BC–448 BC) who was hired to deliver a lyric poem as part of a celebration honoring the host's victory in chariot race. Over the course of Simonides' performance, the host became offended by what he perceived to be excessive praise of the mythological figures Castor and Pollux. As a result, the host paid Simonides only half of the amount agreed upon and suggested that Simonides have Castor and Pollux pay the remainder of the fee. Soon after the confrontation with the host, Simonides was called out of the banquet hall by a pair of visitors. After Simonides left the banquet hall, the roof collapsed inside, killing the host and all of his guests. It was then revealed that the visitors wishing to speak with Simonides were Castor and Pollux, who had arrived to save his life. Later, while recovering the bodies from the disaster site, people determined that the bodies were too disfigured to be identified. However, Simonides was able to recall the location at which each guest was sitting in the banquet hall and thus was able to identify each corpse. On the basis of this experience, Simonides developed a mnemonic system that first involves forming a mental image of a familiar place (Yarmey, 1984). Then, using an ordered arrangement, one mentally places to-be-remembered items in various locations of the imagined familiar place. At the time of recall, one simply revisits the imagined familiar place and retrieves the to-be-remembered items. As will be shown in Chapter 4, this mnemonic technique is now known as the method of loci and is still used today.

Ancient Greek and Roman orators also advocated the use of bizarre mental imagery to enhance memory. The oldest surviving Latin text on rhetoric (*Rhetorica Ad Herennium*) provides a good deal of discourse devoted to instruction on the memorization of speeches. A centerpiece of that instruction is the argument that construction of humorous or ridiculous images in association with to-be-remembered information will maximize the likelihood of retrieving that information from memory (Yates, 1966). It is interesting to note that the use of bizarre imagery is a component of several mnemonic techniques advocated in modern texts on memory and cognitive psychology. Modern research on the mnemonic effectiveness of bizarre imagery will be discussed in Chapter 3.

□ The Middle Ages

The heavy use of mnemonic strategies continued through the Middle Ages. During this time, good memory was highly revered, and mnemonic training was an integral part of the educational system (Carruthers, 1990). Moreover, it is believed that lawyers of this time committed entire sets of laws and codes to memory using a variety of mnemonic techniques (Fentress & Wickham, 1992). Particularly interesting is a translation of the mnemonic techniques advocated by Hugh of St. Victor provided by Carruthers (2002). Like his predecessors, Hugh of St. Victor strongly advocated the use of mental imagery to enhance memory. However, the most striking characteristic of Hugh of St. Victor's instruction is the emphasis that was placed on the organization of to-be-remembered information. Specifically, he used the analogy of the meticulous organization of a money changer who could quickly and without hesitation retrieve the appropriate coins from a pouch that contained numerous coins of different types. It was suggested that information to be remembered should be organized similarly. With rigorous mental organization, the to-be-remembered information would be stored in "distinct locations" in memory and would thus be immune from interference and easily retrieved. Although the method of loci used by ancient orators provided an ordered placement of information within a mental image, Hugh of St. Victor's system appears to be more strongly related to modern organizational mnemonic techniques such as categorical and schematic organization. Modern organizational techniques will be discussed in Chapter 5.

The emphasis on organizational mnemonics as opposed to the more circumscribed method of loci appears to have been a trend in the Middle Ages. According to Carruthers (1990), the method of loci fell out of favor between the first and 12th centuries as it was considered somewhat of a gimmick during that time. In its place, mnemonic techniques such as the use of rhymes began to emerge. Of particular interest is Carruthers's description of a rhyme-based mnemonic technique advocated by John of

Garland. John of Garland suggested that one should make use of similarities between the sounds of unfamiliar and familiar terms in order to enhance memory for the meaning of the unfamiliar terms. This technique is very similar to the modern keyword method that is used to enhance second-language acquisition. The keyword method will be discussed in Chapter 4.

The advocacy of bizarre imagery as a mnemonic remained strong throughout the Middle Ages. Carruthers (1990) illustrated this point in her description of the system offered by Thomas Bradwardine (c. 1290–1349) to memorize the signs of the zodiac. Bradwardine suggested that each symbol of the zodiac should be connected to an adjacent symbol via interactive imagery. For example, Leo, Virgo, Libra, and Scorpio were associated by an image consisting of a bloodied lion (Leo) attacking a beautiful maiden (Virgo) whose arm is extremely swollen from the sting of a scorpion (Scorpio) that the maiden is balancing on her scales (Libra). Carruthers noted that all of Bradwardine's suggested imagery was extreme and that this extremity was "in conformity with a basic principle for memory images, namely, that what is unusual is more memorable than what is routine" (Carruthers, 1990, p. 134). This clearly suggests that bizarreness was the norm for mnemonic imagery in the Middle Ages. It should also be noted that Bradwardine's system bares a striking resemblance to the modern linking-by-story method, which will be discussed in Chapter 5.

☐ The Renaissance

It is widely believed that the method of loci reemerged as a fundamentally important mnemonic during the Renaissance (Carruthers, 1990; Engel, 1991). Given that reference to ancient texts is generally considered a hallmark of the Renaissance, it is not particularly surprising that some of the earliest mnemonics reappeared during this period. However, what is striking is that some thinkers who were not even aware that the method of loci had been covered extensively in ancient texts arrived at the basic principles of the method independently (Engel, 1991). This may have been due in part to an intellectual climate that allowed for a more general acceptance of all mnemonic techniques than had existed previously. Moreover, the humanistic emphasis on mental capabilities may have also spurred additional intellectual thought on the topic of mnemonics (Carruthers, 1990).

Although the use of mnemonics was generally accepted during the Renaissance, English Puritans took issue with imagery-based mnemonics (Couliano, 1987). The Puritans believed that imagery-based mnemonics were idolatrous and that the bizarre imagery often elicited by such techniques was obscene. At the center of this controversy were Alexander Dicson and William Perkins. Dicson was a student of Giordano Bruno's mnemonic system, which was a variation of the method of loci. Bruno's system involved heavy use of mental imagery and was associated with Hermetic occultism (Yates, 1966). Perkins was a theologian and Puritan leader who advocated Petrus Ramus's organizational mnemonic techniques. Thus, the dispute between Dicson and Perkins was just as much about religion as it was about mnemonic techniques. Specifically, as led by Perkins, the Puritans associated imagery-based mnemonics with the occult as well as with the Catholic Church (Couliano, 1987). Making an argument similar to that which they directed at the Catholic Church for the veneration of saints, the Puritans maintained that the use of mental imagery amounted to heresy as it reflected a form of idol worship. Moreover, the Puritans were especially opposed to the use of zodiac symbols in Bruno's mnemonic system (Yates, 1966).

☐ The Introduction of the Scientific Method

In the latter stages of the Renaissance, scholars were less influenced by authoritative sources and began to embrace systematic observation and experimentation as preferred methods for the acquisition of knowledge. Francis Bacon, a major contributor to the development and popularity of these empirical methods, was also a proponent of mnemonic techniques. As noted by Yates (1966), Bacon fully embraced the use of mental imagery to enhance memory. However, Bacon believed that the use of mnemonics by rhetoricians and orators was gimmicky showmanship and that the main value of mnemonics was tied to their potential applications to scientific investigation. For example, Bacon suggested that variations of the method of loci could be used to facilitate invention by making knowledge readily available for creative use (Engel, 1997). In this way, one might consider Bacon's view of mnemonics as a precursor to the use of mnemonics as a tool for educators. The modern use of mnemonics in education will be discussed in Chapter 7.

It should also be noted that Bacon was not an advocate of the use of bizarre imagery (Yates, 1966; Yeo, 2004). Thus, it appears that Bacon's position on mnemonics was a bit of a compromise between classic mnemonic techniques and the imageless organizational mnemonics espoused by the Puritans. Bacon accepted the use of image-based mnemonics such as the method of loci and its variants but suggested that imagery should be sensible and used mainly to structure to-be-remembered information in an orderly fashion.

Despite the qualified acceptance of mnemonics by Francis Bacon, succeeding influential thinkers flatly rejected the use of internal mnemonics and instead advocated the use of external mnemonics. A common thread among those who rejected the use of internal mnemonics was the belief that the memory system was extremely fragile. As a result of this fragility, internal associations among ideas could be easily distorted such that they no longer reflected their natural connections with the world and could possibly even approximate madness (Yeo, 2004). In keeping with this sentiment, John Locke, whose *An Essay Concerning Human Understanding* (1690) marked the beginning of British empiricism (Schultz & Schultz, 1992), advocated the use of an external mnemonic known as a "common-place book" (Yeo, 2004). A commonplace book was a method of study in which to-be-remembered information was summarized in the form of notes written under organized headers. Typically, these notes would include relevant themes and quotations that would serve as cues for the retrieval of learned information. Locke believed that this method allowed one to avoid the supposed pitfalls associated with internal associations and to develop habits that "disciplined" the mind.

By the time of Locke's death, the commonplace method had fallen out of favor, and by the 18th century, it had become a target of intellectual loathing (Yeo, 2004). The main argument against the commonplace method was that it was viewed as the method preferred by those seeking a shortcut to learning. Specifically, it was believed that the method encouraged gist learning rather than deeper understanding. Thus, much like the modern educator who bemoans the use of CliffsNotes by his or her students, scholars of that time believed that the commonplace method facilitated intellectual pretense. Of course, using the commonplace method as a shortcut rather than a way to cue retrieval is clearly inconsistent with Locke's use of the method. Nonetheless, the reputation of the commonplace method deteriorated to the point that by the 19th century, the term *commonplace* was being used to refer to trivial facts, much like the use of the term today (Yeo, 2004).

Notwithstanding the fall from grace of his method, Locke's emphasis on organization, storage, and retrieval was a precursor to some of the fundamental topics studied by modern memory researchers. Moreover, the essential components of the commonplace method are very similar to the modern method of advance organizers that has been used to facilitate memory. The use of advance organizers will be discussed again in Chapter 5.

Despite the movement away from internal mnemonics at the end of the Renaissance, there was at least one influential internal mnemonic devised during this time. Using the pseudonym Stanislaus Mink von Wennsshein, Johann Just Winkelmann developed a phonemic system for remembering numbers that involved substituting letters for numbers (Lorayne, 1957). For example, the number 1 was represented by letters T and D because these letters were written with one down stroke. The number 2 was represented by the letter N because it was written with two down strokes. Similarly, each digit (0–9) was associated with one or more letters. In the original system, only consonants were associated with digits. Once the numbers were coded to consonants, vowels were added to render the letters pronounceable, and in this manner, important numbers such as dates could be converted to more memorable phonemes or even words. The method was later refined by Richard Grey (1730) to also include vowels assigned to numbers. This method—often referred to as the "mnemonic major system" or the "phonetic system"—is related to the modern peg-word method, which will be discussed in Chapter 4.

☐ The Emergence of Memory Science

Among the most important developments to impact scholarly attitudes toward mnemonics was the emergence of empirical research on memory in psychology. That development was initiated single-handedly by Hermann Ebbinghaus, whose 1885 monograph announced the first scientific program of research on memory. Ebbinghaus's broad goal was to adapt Fechner's pioneering methods of mental measurement to memory. The subject matter of memory he took from the British associationists (Boring, 1950). To examine the development of associations in memory uncontaminated by prior experience, Ebbinghaus invented the nonsense syllable to be used as the target material, a tacit admission of the importance of meaning to learning and memory. In keeping with the assumption that frequency of experience is the primary determinant of learning and remembering new material, the principle manipulation used by Ebbinghaus was repetition. For example, one of his experiments (Ebbinghaus, 1885/1964) compared the number of repetitions required to learn 80-syllable stanzas of Lord Byron's epic poem *Don Juan* to the number of repetitions required to learn 80 nonsense syllables. The results indicated that it took nine times more repetitions to learn the nonsense syllables than to learn the meaningful information.

Because of Ebbinghaus's interest in the basic acquisition of memory, the bulk of his experiments were conducted just with nonsense syllables. To further ensure that his observations of associative learning were pure, he did not use any mnemonic techniques to learn the syllables; "there was no attempt to connect the nonsense syllables by the invention of special associations of the mnemotecknik type; learning was carried on solely by the influence of the mere repetitions upon natural memory" (Ebbinghaus, 1885/1964, p. 25). As further insurance against unnatural contamination of the learning process, Ebbinghaus used a rapid rate of presentation and recitation, specifically 2.5 items per second. At such a pace, little in the way of natural language or visual imagery mediators could occur (Slamecka, 1985).

The end result of Ebbinghaus's project was to legitimate the scientific study of memory as well as to rigidify the entire field of human learning for the next 80 years. This latter effect, as argued by Young (1985), began a long hiatus of interest in mnemonic techniques. Human learning became conceptualized as the acquisition of associations through rote repetition. The application of this view diminished interest in the use of mnemonic techniques even though they were known to be effective.

Ebbinghaus's work is discussed in William James's groundbreaking book *Principles of Psychology* (1890), which appeared not long after Ebbinghaus published his manuscript. In his book, James addressed questions of efficiency of learning and improvement in retention, placing much less emphasis on sheer repetition than did Ebbinghaus. Specifically, he argued that considering to-be-remembered information in systematic relations with other information provides more cues to assist remembering than simple repetition. This argument directly links elaboration at encoding with cues necessary for retrieval. The notion of the interdependence of encoding and retrieval remains widely accepted today and will be discussed further in Chapter 3.

Besides discussing the essential processes of memory, James (1890) also addressed the topic of improving memory. Specifically, James described three classes of methods used to improve memory: mechanical methods, judicious methods, and ingenious methods. Mechanical methods involve encodings through multiple modalities. For example, James suggested that memory can be improved by hearing, seeing, speaking, and writing the information to be remembered. These methods capture the essence of modern multiple-code theories such as Paivio's (1971, 1991) dual-coding theory (see Chapter 3). As described by James, judicious methods are organizational techniques that emphasize categorization. Although James did not distinguish between external and internal mnemonics, we can assume that this class of methods included the Puritan-endorsed Ramus method as well as the external mnemonics advocated by Descartes and Locke. Ingenious methods were formal mnemonic systems. James described only one ingenious method—a phonetic number system identical to that put forth by Stanislaus Mink von Wennsshein. Interestingly, this system is described by James as the most well-known and most frequently used ingenious method. Thus, when Ebbinghaus's work was first introduced in the United States, mnemonic techniques were still considered to be respectable methods for acquiring and retaining new material. Indeed, much of the focus at that time was on improving memory. However, as the century turned, Ebbinghaus's influence led to mnemonic techniques falling out of favor again (Young, 1985).

☐ Mnemonics Devalued

Events of the early 20th century coalesced to diminish the seriousness with which mnemonics were taken. Most important, the discipline of rhetoric began its demise from the standard university curriculum. For centuries, rhetoric had been the core of liberal studies, and mnemonics was an integral component of rhetoric (Yates, 1966). A principal goal of rhetoric was to train students in the construction and delivery of effective oral argument. Mnemonics training supported this mission by teaching students artificial techniques to remember the structure and details of their arguments. By the last decade of the 19th century, the perceived need to provide dedicated education to oral argument was waning. The discipline of rhetoric began to splinter. Some topics such as logic and critical analysis were absorbed into the curricula of departments of English, philosophy, and mathematics (Kinneavy, 1990). Others, mnemonic training included, lost their place in the curriculum altogether. Before long, the common view of mnemonic techniques changed such that they were no longer considered a respected component of rhetoric. Instead, they were viewed as gimmicks used to support pretentious memory tricks.

Two distinct developments in psychology converged to abet the fall of mnemonics from academic grace. The first of these was the spreading influence of Ebbinghaus's ideas. Young (1985) argued that the success of Ebbinghaus's work became a negative influence on interest in mnemonics. In particular according to Young, Ebbinghaus's focus on the importance of repetition for the development of associations was quickly applied to psychology's functional interest in improving the efficiency of learning and memory. Whereas we have seen that James encouraged the use of mnemonics, it was not long before some of his prominent students such as Angell and Thorndike[1] actively discouraged mnemonic techniques for serious learning. Specifically, Angell described them as "catchpenny" and unacceptably narrow in their usefulness. In many ways, Angell's criticism of mnemonics was similar to the criticism that was levied by intellectuals in the Middle Ages and in the latter stages of the Renaissance—that formal mnemonic systems are gimmicks. Thorndike (1907) said that the only sure route to learning and permanent memory was through repetition; he never mentioned the use of mnemonic strategies. Colvin (1911) was more pointed: "That which was first mastered by tricks of memory must be later comprehended else the learning is worse than useless" (p. 172; as cited by Young, 1985, p. 492).

In the early 20th century, psychology in the United States was closely watched by the education community. Educators were interested in the best ways to facilitate efficient learning, and what better place to look for advice than to the science that proclaimed its interest in the "laws of learning"? The dominant theme from experimental psychology was that learning developed only after substantial repetition. In this climate, the product of mnemonic devices was not considered learning. Young's (1985) provocative argument is that the success of Ebbinghaus's research changed the question from one of how to learn more efficiently to one of how learning occurs. That change effectively replaced mnemonics with repetition and ushered in the era of rote drill in education.

The second influence from psychology that accelerated the demise of mnemonics was the behaviorist manifesto of John Watson (1914). The motivating rationale of behaviorism was that mental concepts should play no role in the scientific analysis of behavior. Among other things, the success of behaviorism eliminated discussion of imagery from psychological research and its application. Mnemonics had inextricable ties to imagery from its very outset, and the neglect of imagery in psychology was tantamount to neglecting mnemonics. It would be 50 years after Watson's initiative before the tenor of American psychology would again favor the study of imagery and with it mnemonics.

In summary, several factors converged in the late 19th and early 20th centuries to reduce the respectability of mnemonics and eliminate it from the standard university curriculum. The diaspora of rhetoric was a fundamental blow. As long as the purpose of rhetoric was held in high esteem, mnemonics would be secure, but with the decreased perceived need for trained orators, mnemonic techniques lost their place in academics and took on the aura of circus tricks. Developments in psychology furthered the decline. The emphasis on developing laws of learning pushed aside interest in facilitating the efficiency of learning, and as repetition settled in as the fundamental law of learning, mnemonic devices took on an even bawdier reputation. Powerful influences in American psychology advocated the banishment of mental concepts from the scientific analyses, and acceptance of that edict removed not just mnemonics but all of memory from active research. In the wake of these influences, research devoted to the analysis of existing mnemonic techniques and development of new ones languished.

☐ Times Get Better

As barren as the early-20th-century scene was for mnemonics research, the sparse work that was done was encouraging in that the emphasis was on empirical examination of the efficiency of specific techniques. This focus appeared as early as 1918 with a paper by David Hill in the *Psychological Bulletin*. Hill advocated the use of specific mnemonic techniques in the classroom to allow "a right evaluation of the mnemonic principle is made possible" (p. 103). The mnemonic used in his study was constructed by his laboratory but was heavily influenced by the mnemonic major system and is nearly identical to the modern peg-word system.

Hill's mnemonic involved the systematic association of words with numbers such that a mnemonic list with words representing the numbers 1 to 100 is memorized. This mnemonic list is then used as a framework to remember succeeding lists. For example, in Hill's list, the word *air* represented the number 1, and *bar* represented the number 2. According to instructions, when presented with the first word of a to-be-remembered list, the learner would form a mental image that associates the word with the first word of the mnemonic list. So, if the first word on the to-be-remembered list was *dog*, the learner might form a mental image of a dog sniffing the air. At the time of recall, the learner simply retrieves the mnemonic list, which has already been committed to memory. Each word on the mnemonic list should then cue the retrieval of the to-be-remembered words as a result of the association formed by the mental image. Although Hill did not report quantitative data in his article, he did state that the system allowed him to successfully recall a 30-item list after a 24-hour retention interval. Hill also stated that the value of the demonstration was that "success upon the part of practically every student was obtained in class work" (p. 103).

Hill's (1918) demonstration also marks the first tacit acceptance of the mnemonic benefits of bizarre imagery to appear in a published journal article. Specifically, Hill stated that vivid imagery, even if it is ridiculous, will allow a learner to remember numerous words presented only once. Hill's work, however, is a rare example in the early to mid-20th century.

To determine the prevalence of mnemonic research in the 20th century, we examined the number of published articles generated by a popular academic database using either the keyword *mnemonic* or *memory aid*. Then, as a crude index of centrality, we computed the number of articles generated by our keywords per 1,000 publications in the area of memory. The results for each decade are depicted in Figure 1.1. The figure indicates a steep decline in the centrality of the discussion of mnemonics beginning in the 1930s and reaching its nadir in the 1950s. These were the halcyon days of behaviorism.

By the middle of the 1950s, a change was building that would lead to a renaissance of cognitive psychology (see Lachman, Lachman, & Butterfield, 1979). The new zeitgeist would be much more hospitable to mnemonics as was evident from a classic paper from the beginning of this cognitive renaissance. In his famous "magic number 7" paper, Miller (1956) reported the case of Sidney Smith's use of mnemonics to code digits and increase his performance on a span test. Importantly, Miller urged the reader to view mnemonic devices not as tricks but as important recoding devices that increase functional memory capacity. Coding

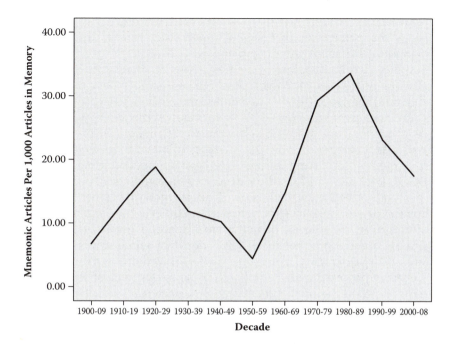

FIGURE 1.1   The number of mnemonic articles per 1,000 articles published in the area of memory by decade.

was destined to become a core concept in learning and memory (Hunt, 2008), and casting mnemonics as an aid to coding was an important step toward its rehabilitation. Indeed, the data in Figure 1.1 show that the number of papers on mnemonics increased through the 1960s into the 1980s, mirroring psychology's general return to topics of cognition. However, the increased activity in mnemonic research would not keep pace with the continued upswing in research activity in memory and cognition. As shown in Figure 1.1, mnemonic research as indexed by publications has experienced a sharp decline since 1980. One has to wonder why, in such a favorable intellectual milieu and with so much attention directed to memory, that so little is being done with mnemonics.

☐ Mnemonics and the Scientific Study of Memory

Although we cannot identify with certainty the causes for the relative lack of research on mnemonics in contemporary psychology, suspicion falls on several factors. Among these are hangovers from our earlier discussion such as the perception that formal mnemonics is a set of techniques designed to artificially enhance memory, with little purpose other than to produce gimmicky tricks of memory. Another persisting impediment is that the goal of psychological research on memory continues to be to understand the processes, not to increase the efficiency of those processes. Several more recent developments have widened the gap between the science of memory and traditional mnemonics. Current conceptualizations of natural memory minimize the necessity of intent to remember for successful memory. A lasting influence of the levels of processing framework (Craik & Lockhart, 1972) is the assumption that memory is a by-product of perception and comprehension. That is, memory comes for free in the wake of our normal experiences; remembering an experience does not require or necessarily benefit from intending to remember it. This assumption about how memory works does not segue smoothly into the intentional use of formal mnemonic devices in order to remember.

Levels of processing also emphasized the importance of semantic processing for good memory. Processing of surface information was associated with poor retention. On the one hand, this emphasis counters the historical focus on repetition that began with Ebbinghaus and culminated with the emphasis on rote rehearsal for transfer from short-term to long-term memory. On the other hand, the emphasis on semantic processing converges with research on comprehension to conclude that the normal memory product is the meaning or gist of an experience. Formal mnemonics almost always has the goal of yielding verbatim memory. This discrepancy between the assumptions and conclusions from scientific psychology about the operation of normal memory and the target application for mnemonic techniques increases the perception of mnemonics as out of touch with the important function of memory.

Another potential factor in the neglect of mnemonics by scientific psychology is the explosion of interest in false memory over the past 20 years. Beginning with Roediger and McDermott's (1995) influential paper, research has highlighted the fallibility of human memory and turned significant amounts of effort toward memory errors. An important discovery in this research is that false memory results, in many instances, from the normal operation of comprehension. Against this backdrop, mnemonics, with its emphasis on precision and accuracy of memory, again finds itself at odds with the prevailing zeitgeist of memory research.

Memory research concentrates on the operation of natural memory processes, and mnemonics, which by definition is artificial, remains largely outside the purview of that research. Meanwhile, the demands for artificial uses of memory have not abated. The development of technology whose function is in large part to reduce or replace demands on human cognition has added significantly to the burden of verbatim memory.

Books and journals are being found more easily on the Internet than at a library, letters and memos are being replaced by e-mail, paper money has given way to bank cards, and purchases are often made in front of a computer rather than at a store. These changes are not the result of a passing fad but an indication of a trend that will continue throughout the century. And what do all of these changes have in common? Each of the changes mentioned place increased demands on memory. Separate passwords and usernames are often needed for accessing books online, for sending e-mail, for accessing bank records, and for making financial transactions. Moreover, problems that have not been encountered at other points in history such as identity theft and computer hijacking require that we make our usernames and passwords as difficult and personally unrevealing as possible. As a result, the memorization of nearly random strings of digits and letters has become a necessity of modern life. Importantly, these demands on memory are in addition to the myriad things we need to commit to memory that are unrelated to our new dependence on information processing technology.

Our goal for this book is to begin a rapprochement between the traditional purpose of mnemonics and the study of natural human memory in scientific psychology.

What we have in mind is a serious effort to bring the best of science to bear on improving memory but as well to subject the best of mnemonics to scientific analysis. The effort goes beyond what is traditionally considered mnemonics in that we intend to exploit any opening offered by memory research to facilitate memory, including the development of individual strategies tailored for specific needs. Because the word mnemonics denotes a very clear set of practices, many of which are arguably disdained by scientific psychology, we propose to name our endeavor mnemonology. We recommend this new terminology with all due modesty and for two principal reasons. First, we intend to broaden the scope of the exercise beyond what people usually think of as mnemonics, and adding the new term is easier than asking people to redefine their long-standing interpretation of what mnemonics means. Second, mnemonology captures a meaning that is closer to our goal than does the term mnemonics. We close the first chapter with a brief discussion of that difference.

☐ From Mnemonology to Mnemonics and Back

The relative neglect of mnemonics by memory science likely reflects the fact that formal mnemonic systems are as removed from the scientific view of normal memory today as was the "mnemotecknik" from Ebbinghaus's emphasis on repetition. For most people, the meaning of mnemonics is exhausted by the techniques of formal mnemonics, but, in fact, the definition is "a memory aid" or, for those preferring a dictionary definition, "a technique of improving the memory" (*Merriam-Webster Collegiate Dictionary*, 2007). Thus, the true meaning of the word *mnemonics* is not captured by a set of formal procedures.

Basic memory research has made substantial progress in isolating processes fundamental to the operation of memory, and one could imagine that successful mnemonic techniques engage combinations of these processes. Importantly, the relevant cognitive processes can be activated by an almost infinite number of operations. Thus, theoretically, there are unlimited possibilities for the creation of successful new methods for enhancing memory. However, according to the narrow definition of mnemonics, these methods might not even be classified as mnemonics, and thus they could be lost in the chasm that often exists between the academic researcher and the consumer of scientific knowledge.

Perhaps the affiliation between memory science and mnemonics can be strengthened by explicitly recognizing the portion of memory research that successfully identifies processes that facilitate memory. We suggest that this area of interest in basic research be called *mnemonology*. With the identification of those processes, techniques to aid memory could be developed from the basic research. Thus, mnemonology would yield mnemonics. Moreover, mnemonology would include analysis of existing mnemonic techniques both for their effectiveness in various settings and for their underlying psychological mechanisms. In this regard, a mnemonological analysis of mnemonics would contribute to the development of basic theory in memory science.

For example, it has been suggested that, for many mnemonics, a combination of the processes of elaboration and organization is required for effectiveness (Worthen & Hunt, 2008). The method of loci involves a component that encourages elaboration, a component that encourages organization, and a component that encourages both elaboration and organization. Does this mean that one or more of the components of the ancient system are superfluous? If so, the method could be tested using a dismantling design to determine the components necessary for mnemonic effectiveness. The value of such research would be the possibility of a reduction in the complexity of the method, which would ultimately make it more user friendly. Research such as this not only could be conducted but should be conducted for each formal mnemonic.

As mentioned earlier in the chapter, our approach to mnemonics emphasizes the processes that underlie mnemonics rather than provides circumscribed instructions for mnemonic effectiveness. Our rationale for this approach is that if one understands the basic processes underlying mnemonic devices, then one should be able to generate a variety of simple mnemonics techniques for himself or herself. These self-generated mnemonics would have the advantage of complementing individual learning styles and objectives. Needless to say, it is unlikely that people would create a mnemonic for their own use that they would consider gimmicky or otherwise a waste of time. The creation of new mnemonics could also result in mnemonic systems that are effective for remembering a broad range of knowledge by a variety of users. Moreover, with the mnemonological approach to mnemonics, the research laboratory could be used both to test existing mnemonics and to develop new, user-friendly techniques that have broad applications (cf. Henshel, 1980).

By adopting the mnemonology advocated here, the downward trend in research conducted in the area of mnemonics during the past two decades has the potential to be reversed quickly and easily. The reason being is that although mnemonic research has declined, research on processes related to memory improvement is and has always been central to the study of memory. As such, the revival of mnemonic research need not rely on researchers with a background in mnemonics or mnemonic instruction. Rather, the future of mnemonic research lies with researchers interested in the applications of basic memory processes.

In summary, we all depend on our memory throughout the course of our day—just like the hunter-gatherers of the Upper Paleolithic, the ancient Greeks and Romans, the inhabitants of the Medieval and Renaissance periods, and all of the critics of mnemonic techniques. The point is that humans rely on memory to negotiate their daily lives, and as long as they continue to do so, there will always be an interest in improving memory. It is our hope that our efforts here will inspire additional research on mnemonics and revive the ancient art of memory.

General Considerations in Selecting Mnemonics

Mnemonics are useful in almost any situation in which learning and memory are the goals, but one size does not fit all. The effectiveness of a mnemonic requires that the technique be matched to the particular circumstances of application. The rub is that the particular circumstances can differ in countless ways. For example, one simply might want to commit a 12-item grocery list to memory. Then again one might want to learn to play Rachmaninoff's Piano Concerto no. 2. The same technique is unlikely to be equally effective in these circumstances. Given the goal of fitting the mnemonic to the circumstances, it would be helpful if we can specify dimensions to consider when selecting a mnemonic. In this chapter we discuss some of the more important of those dimensions as identified by basic memory research in conjunction with practical considerations. For example, we have good reason to believe that the processes underlying memory for particular events differ from the processes underlying the acquisition of knowledge. We also know that different kinds of memory tests are differentially sensitive to different kinds of learning. Individual differences among people must be taken into account when selecting a strategy for a particular individual. What works for you may or may not work for me. Another important consideration is who creates the mnemonic, the user or someone else. Each of these concerns will crop up periodically throughout the book in various contexts. Consequently we shall devote the chapter to a general description of these issues as they relate to the selection of mnemonic techniques for particular situations.

☐ Type of Memory

The kind of memory that is to be established is an important consideration in selecting a proper mnemonic. Here we briefly describe "kind" of memory on two separate dimensions. The first involves the type of representation to be established, either a context-dependent or a context-independent representation. This distinction corresponds to the difference between memory and knowledge. The second distinction is between retrospective and prospective memory. This distinction captures the difference between remembering an event in the past versus remembering to do something in the future. The kinds of memory on both of these dimensions respond differently to different cues, and effective mnemonics will differ across these dimensions.

Memory Versus Knowledge

When deciding which mnemonic is most appropriate for a given learning situation, one must first consider what type of memory will be accessed at the time of retrieval. According to Tulving (1985), there are two basic types of memory that are represented in separate memory systems. Episodic memory consists of memories for specific, time-dated events and experiences. For example, where you went on your most recent vacation, what you ordered the last time you ate at a Thai restaurant, and who was the opening act at the Nickelback concert you attended are all considered episodic memories. These events represent specific episodes that occurred at specific times and within a specific context. In contrast, semantic memory reflects general knowledge that is not tied to a specific time-dated episode. Knowing that blue and yellow make green, that the basenji is the only breed of dog that does not bark, and that work = force × distance would each be considered semantic memories. It is important to note that episodic and semantic memories are encoded simultaneously but are believed to be stored separately. For example, consider a situation in which, while reading a book on an airplane traveling from Seattle to Houston, one learns that the Native American Chitimacha tribe once inhabited the area now known as New Orleans. Knowledge of the relationship between the Chitimacha tribe and New Orleans is represented in semantic memory. However, the information about how (from a particular book) and when (during a trip from Seattle to Houston) the knowledge was acquired is represented in episodic memory.

In addition to episodic and semantic memories, Tulving (1985) described procedural memories, which are thought to be stored in a subsystem of the semantic memory system. Procedural knowledge includes memory for learned procedures and skills. Knowledge pertaining to riding a bicycle, shooting a free throw, and peeling an apple are examples of procedural memories.

For the present purposes, it is important to note that each of the memory types described differ in terms of how they are best remembered. The retrieval of episodic memories is enhanced by cues specific to the context in which the event occurred. That is, an episodic event is most likely to be recalled from memory when a retrieval cue that was encoded along with the to-be-remembered event is used (Tulving, 1972). For example, when trying to remember where you went on your first date, information about who accompanied you on that date would be helpful to the retrieval of the location. Given the importance of context to episodic memory, the most appropriate mnemonics to use for remembering episodic information are those that enhance the encoding of specific contextual cues during learning.

Because semantic memories are not bound to a specific context, cue specificity is less important for retrieval in semantic memory. Rather, semantic memory depends on associations with preexisting knowledge structures. As such, a student who is trying to remember who established the first journal in psychology is unlikely to benefit from being told that she read the information in her introductory psychology textbook while at the library on September 5, 2007. However, when cued with associated information such as the fact that the person who established the first journal also established the first psychological laboratory, the student is far more likely to remember that the answer is Wilhelm Wundt. Thus, mnemonics that emphasize associations with previously stored knowledge are more effective for semantic memories than those that emphasize context-specific cues.

Procedural memories are thought to be retrieved and utilized without conscious awareness (Tulving, 1985). Furthermore, conscious awareness of procedural information can interfere with performance of a skill. Consider the case of a guitarist giving a solo performance of a difficult composition. If he were to attend to the specific movements of his fingers and hands required to play each note rather than devoting his attention to the resulting melody, his performance would almost certainly suffer. Thus, in most cases, procedural memories do not require conscious retrieval at all. However, that is not to say that mnemonics are not relevant to procedural memories. Mnemonics that enhance encoding by reinforcing the behaviors associated with a given procedure will ultimately enhance performance even without conscious retrieval.

Retrospective and Prospective Memory

Another distinction to consider when choosing an appropriate mnemonic is whether the memory to be enhanced is retrospective or prospective in nature. Retrospective memory involves recalling information that has been learned previously such as directions to a friend's house. Prospective memory involves remembering to do something in the future such as remembering to take the bottle of wine you promised to bring to your friend's house. Although retrospective memory has been researched much more extensively than prospective memory, both types of memory are important, and they are interdependent. Consider an older person who has been prescribed several daily medications. Not only must she remember to take each medication at the appropriate time, but she must also remember where the medications are located. If prospective memory fails, then the person forgets to take the medicine at the appropriate time, and her health could be jeopardized. If she remembers to take the medication at the appropriate time but cannot remember where she last placed it, then the result is the same: The necessary medication is not taken.

Prospective memory failure—sometimes referred to as absentminded forgetting (Schacter & Wiseman, 2006)—can be especially problematic when attention is divided among several different tasks. Moreover, if the intended task competes with a highly scripted or routinized task, then forgetting is even more likely (Hay & Jacoby, 1996; Sellen, 1994). For example, consider a person whose daily routine involves working until 4:30 p.m., working out at the gym from 4:45 to 5:30, and then driving a particular route that will bring her home just in time to eat dinner that has been prepared by her husband. This person will be far more likely to forget to pick up hamburger buns on the way home than a person whose routine is more variable.

Consideration of whether a situation involves a retrospective memory, a prospective memory, or both is an important factor for determining an appropriate mnemonic. In general, memory improves when the mnemonic used creates a strong association between the specific task to be performed and the appropriate time and context in which the task is to be performed (Engelkamp, 1998). In addition, mnemonics that provide unusual or distinctive cues can be especially helpful (McDaniel & Einstein, 1993). Importantly, both retrospective and prospective memory tasks may benefit from both factors.

☐ Test Factors

There are numerous situations in which people may rely on mnemonics to improve memory. Often these situations differ in terms of what sort of information must be recovered from memory. A major demarcation is that between recognition and recall. Recognition requires a decision about a particular prior experience, whereas recall requires reproduction of the experience in some form. Within recall, a variety of different types of information and test environments can influence performance. Thus, it is important to consider the demands a particular situation places on the memory system when choosing an appropriate mnemonic.

Recall

Free Recall. One of the most difficult memory situations involves a test of free recall. When free recall is tested, one must retrieve target information without the aid of external cues or with cues that are extremely general. Imagine having attended a party over the weekend, and upon returning to work on Monday morning, you are asked remember all who were in attendance. This test requires proper encoding of information about the attendees, storage of the information in a way that is easily accessible, and retrieval with the benefit of only internally generated cues. Thus, free recall involves three fundamental memory processes: encoding, storage, and retrieval. To successfully enhance free recall, a mnemonic must include procedures that strengthen each of these processes. However, as will be discussed in Chapter 3, any procedure that affects encoding will also influence retrieval. So, a mnemonic need not include separate procedures for each of the fundamental processes. On the other hand, it should be noted that purely organizational mnemonics (e.g., schema and category organizational schemes) are likely to result in a high number of recall intrusions.

Serial Recall. Serial recall is a form of free recall in which target information must be recalled in a specified order. For example, when attempting to remember how to make seafood gumbo in the absence of a recipe, one must remember all of the necessary ingredients as well ordered steps for the combination of ingredients. Either failure to remember all of the ingredients or failure to recall the steps in the correct order could negatively affect the taste of the gumbo. Indeed, a preparation of seafood gumbo that does not begin with a good roux is considered sacrilege in some parts of the United States! In this example, remembering the ingredients would involve free recall, but remembering the order of inclusion of the ingredients would involve serial recall. The processes that govern serial recall are similar to the processes that govern free recall. However, serial recall is far more dependent on the organizational process than is free recall. As such, a successful mnemonic for situations in which serial recall is tested must include encoding procedures that strongly enhance the organizational structure of the to-be-remembered information. Perhaps as a result of the relative difficulty of this type of memory test, several formal mnemonics have been devised to enhance serial recall.

Cued Recall. In a cued recall test, the learner is provided with a cue to aid retrieval of the target information at the time of testing. One may be tempted to assume that cued recall is always easier than free recall. However, cued recall success varies widely with the quality and appropriateness of the provided cue. As mentioned earlier, a contextual cue will not facilitate retrieval of a semantic memory as well as it might facilitate an episodic memory. In addition, some cues can even have an inhibitory effect on retrieval.

A study by Brown (1979) provides a good demonstration of an inhibitory effect in cued recall. In that study, participants were presented with definitions of words with a relatively low frequency of occurrence. Following each definition, a semantically related cue, an orthographically related cue, or an unrelated cue was provided for the retrieval of the target word. The results indicated that orthographic cues facilitated recall, but semantic cues inhibited recall. Similarly, Roediger, Stellon, and Tulving (1977) found that cueing recall of a list of words with items from the target list inhibited recall relative to free recall of the list. The results of both studies can be explained by the fact that the cues causing inhibition in each study were very similar to the information to be recalled. High similarity between a cue and target information can result in activation that leads to competition between the cue and the target at the time of retrieval. As such, the retrieval of target information can be blocked by the related information—a situation referred to as an "ugly sister effect" (Reason & Lucas, 1984). The problem of inhibitory cues underscores the importance of choosing a mnemonic, which results in a highly discriminable memory representation when cued recall will be tested. For example, mnemonics that capitalize on distinctive processing or imaginal elaboration at encoding would be safe bets for enhancing cued recall.

It is also important to note that mnemonics that are effective in enhancing free recall do not necessarily improve cued recall performance and vice versa. For example, Wollen and Cox (1981) demonstrated that the mnemonic effectiveness of bizarre imagery depends on the type of memory test. Specifically, their results indicated that bizarre imagery was more effective than common imagery in improving free recall but that common imagery was more effective than bizarre imagery when cued recall was tested. It should be noted, however, that this pattern of results can be moderated by other variables (see the Retention Interval section).

Recognition

In a test of recognition, the learner is presented with an item and asked to determine whether it had been present in the learning situation. As such, a recognition test includes some previously learned information and some information that is new relative to the to-be-learned information. A situation in which a person must identify a perpetrator from a police lineup is an example of a recognition test. In this situation, the perpetrator may or may not be present within the lineup. Thus, correct recognition involves determining whether each person in the lineup matches the representation of the perpetrator stored in memory. Notice that successful recognition depends less on the retrieval of target information than recall,[2] because in the former case the item to be assessed is presented at testing whereas in the latter case it is not. Thus, like those appropriate for cued recall, mnemonics used for situations in which recognition memory is tested should include procedures that maximize the discriminability of the memory representation.

Recognition is often assumed to be easier than recall. However, high similarity between the to-be-remembered target and nontarget distractors (foils or lures) can make recognition more difficult than recall. Moreover, the existence of such similarities can result in a high level of misidentification. On the other hand, a blatant lack of similarity among foils can also increase the possibility of misidentification (Loftus, 1979). For example, if the perpetrator of a crime is described as having a tattoo and the lineup includes mainly foils without tattoos, the probability of mistakenly identifying a tattooed foil from the lineup is greater than the probability of identifying the same tattooed foil from a lineup in which all suspects have tattoos. Needless to say, the mistaken identification of an innocent person as a perpetrator could have devastating consequences. This possibility further underscores the importance of mnemonics that lead to highly discriminable memory traces for situations in which recognition memory will be tested.

The influence of decision-making processes on recognition memory is another factor to consider when selecting an appropriate mnemonic. Tanner and Swets (1954) developed a theory of the detection of target stimuli that is especially relevant to recognition-memory judgments. Applied to recognition, this theory suggests the recognition judgments are influenced by both the discriminability of the to-be-remembered information and the decision-making processes. For example, if the rewards for correct recognition outweigh the costs of misidentifications, then the decision-making threshold lowers, resulting in an increase in both correct identifications and misidentifications. Going back to our example of a police lineup, high reward and low cost would increase the likelihood of identifying the perpetrator. However, it would also increase the probability that the witness misidentifies an innocent suspect from the lineup. This pattern—known as a liberal response bias—reflects a lower threshold of evidence required for identification. Conversely, if costs outweigh rewards, then more evidence is required for a positive identification. This is known as a conservative response bias. These biases are an important consideration because some mnemonic strategies are designed specifically to reduce recognition bias.

McAllister, Bearden, Kohlmaier, and Warner (1997) provided an example of an external mnemonic designed to reduce bias. These authors examined factors that could influence identification of a perpetrator using a mug book procedure. Specifically, they examined the possibility that a computerized mug book that includes dynamic suspect characteristics such as voice and gait could reduce the number of misidentifications of innocent suspects. Participants in this study watched a videotaped crime and then viewed one of three types of mug books: a computerized mug book that always included dynamic information, a mug book that made dynamic information available if the participant chose to examine it, or a mug book that contained no dynamic information. The results indicated that mug books that made dynamic information available if the participant wished to examine it resulted in fewer misidentifications than mug books that did not include dynamic information. Importantly, the decrease in misidentifications occurred without a corresponding decrease in the number of correct identifications. This suggests that the additional cues provided by the dynamic information led to a reduction in liberal responding.

Retention Interval

Another important factor to consider when choosing a mnemonic is the amount of time that will elapse between learning and the memory test. Indeed, some researchers (e.g., Wang & Thomas, 2000) have suggested that the ability to improve memory over an extended period of time is an important litmus test for determining the overall effectiveness of a mnemonic. Importantly, some mnemonics enhance memory at short retention intervals but not at long intervals. Other mnemonics are effective after long retention intervals but not after short ones.

Research by Krinsky and Krinsky (1994, 1996) suggests that the effectiveness of the peg-word method may fluctuate depending on the length of the retention interval. Specifically, these authors examined the effectiveness of the peg-word method as a technique for improving serial recall of verbal material among fifth graders. The results of both studies indicated better recall for those who were trained to use the peg-word method relative to untrained controls when memory was tested immediately. However, after a 48-hour delay, the peg-word method did not improve memory relative to the control condition.

On the other hand, some mnemonics are more effective after a delay than when memory is tested immediately. Earlier in this chapter, we suggested that common imagery is more effective than bizarre imagery when cued recall is tested. However, research has shown that this effect is moderated by the length of retention interval. Specifically, O'Brien and Wolford (1982) found that although there were no significant differences between imagery types after a short delay, bizarre imagery led to significantly better cued recall performance than common imagery after a 1-week retention interval.

As the example of bizarre imagery demonstrates, numerous situational factors determine the effectiveness of a given mnemonic. A mnemonic may be very effective in some situations but not at all effective in others. As such, an arsenal of mnemonics may be necessary to obtain consistent memory enhancement across different testing situations.

☐ Individual Differences

Differences in Aptitude

The effectiveness of mnemonic techniques also varies among individuals. As an example, Griffith and Actkinson (1978) demonstrated that the effectiveness of the peg-word method was related to general aptitude. In this study, general aptitude was measured using the arithmetic reasoning and verbal subscales of the Armed Services Vocational Aptitude Battery. Participants representing high, medium, and low aptitude either received no instructions or were instructed in the use of the peg-word method prior to learning three lists of digit–noun associations. The results indicated that only the high-aptitude participants benefited from the mnemonic training. On the basis of these results, one might argue that the peg-word method is useful for only a minority of the population. However, a more likely explanation is that the medium- and low-aptitude participants had more difficulty using the method as instructed than did the high-aptitude participants. Regardless, the results of this study are consistent with the notion that mnemonics with numerous or complicated procedures are unlikely to be immediately and effectively utilized by unskilled learners.

It may also be the case that learners with strong verbal abilities have an easier time employing even simple mnemonics than do those with lesser ability. Indeed, previous research suggests that individuals with strong vocabularies are better at generating elaboration and forming associations than individuals with weak vocabularies (Kyllonen, Tirre, & Christal, 1991). Moreover, the elaboration produced by high-ability individuals is generally more effective than elaboration produced by low-ability individuals (Wang, 1983).

The relationship between aptitude and mnemonics described above may lead one to believe that mnemonics may be ineffective for those who need them most. However, this is not the case. Although it is true that high-aptitude individuals may learn and benefit from mnemonics more rapidly than those displaying low aptitude, research suggests that learners at nearly any level of ability, given enough learning time and proper instruction, can benefit from even formal mnemonics (Bellezza, 1996). Regardless, it is likely that mnemonics with complicated procedures are especially cumbersome for low-aptitude learners. This issue will loom very large when we take up the discussion of mnemonics in cognitive rehabilitation in Chapter 8.

Personality Differences

Very little work is available on the relationship between personality variables and mnemonic effectiveness. However, the existing research suggests that personality differences may influence the effectiveness of some mnemonics. For example, Moss, Worthen, Haydel, Mac Mahon, and Savoy (2008) examined relationships among several personality variables and the effectiveness of bizarre imagery in enhancing free recall. The results indicated that high arousal-seeking tendency and high conservatism were each related to increased effectiveness of bizarre imagery. However, it is important to note that participants in this study did not generate their own bizarre and common elaboration but instead were asked to form mental images based on provided sentences (half bizarre and half common). Thus, it is not clear whether these personality variables would also be related to the mnemonic effectiveness of self-generated elaboration. Also, the authors suggested that the relationship between conservatism and the effectiveness of bizarre elaboration was related to a defensive response to bizarreness. Thus, it may be that individuals high in conservatism would be unlikely to willingly choose a mnemonic that incorporates the use of bizarre elaboration. Nonetheless, at the very least, this study shows that individual differences may govern the effectiveness of mnemonics that incorporate bizarre elaboration when such mnemonics are imposed upon learners by an external source (e.g., an instructor in a classroom).

In a similar vein, Cimbalo, Clark, and Matayev (2003) examined the relationship between sensation seeking and the isolation effect. The isolation effect refers to enhanced memory for an item that differs from all other to-be-remembered items on some noticeable dimension. The results indicated that high sensation seeking was related to an increased isolation effect with a 10-second simultaneous presentation of list items but not with a 2-second presentation. Although these results may have implications for the use of distinctiveness-based mnemonics, they are inconsistent with previous research (Gratzinger, Sheikh, Friedman, & Yesavage, 1990; Moss et al., 2008; Zoller, Workman, & Kroll, 1989), which has failed to find a significant relationship between sensation seeking and mnemonic effectiveness.

Two studies involving older adults (Finkel & Yesavage, 1989; Gratzinger et al., 1990) found a relationship between openness to experience and memory improvement that is dependent on the method of instruction used during mnemonic training. Openness to experience is a personality variable that differentiates between people who are open to new experiences and those who prefer more familiar experiences (Costa & McCrae, 1976). Finkel and Yesavage found a significant positive relationship between openness to experience and memory improvement among older participants who received computer-aided instruction in the use of the method of loci. However, openness to experience was not related to memory improvement for participants who received standard instruction. In addition, Gratzinger et al. found a significant relationship between the fantasy subscale of the openness to experience scale and memory improvement after certain methods of mnemonic training. The fantasy subscale measures the extent to which one is imaginative and has an active fantasy life. Thus, it is not surprising that high fantasy scores were related to greater benefit from mnemonic training when that training was supplemented with imagery training. However, when the mnemonic training was supplemented with relaxation training, high fantasy scores were related to less mnemonic benefit.

As a general statement, learners should choose mnemonics that fit well their own personal learning style and abilities. For example, highly visual learners may benefit most from imagery-based mnemonics. On the other hand, primarily auditory learners may benefit most from rhyme-based mnemonics. Regardless of learning style and ability, one should always select a mnemonic that is comfortable and allows one to enter into a learning situation with confidence.

☐ Internal Versus External Mnemonics

In Chapter 1, we defined an external mnemonic as a cue placed in the environment in order to improve memory. An internal mnemonic was defined as a cognitive strategy designed to enhance the encoding of information and, as a result, may enhance storage and retrieval. Although the processes that underlie internal mnemonics are the primary focus of this book, external mnemonics are widely used and quite effective in some circumstances.

Distinguishing Mnemonics From Records

First, we wish to draw a distinction between an external mnemonic and a record of to-be-remembered information. A written grocery list that

TABLE 2.1 Full List of Grocery Items and a Condensed Mnemonic List

Grocery List	Mnemonic List
Tomatoes	Stuff for spaghetti dinner
Mushrooms	Breakfast foods
Noodles	Toiletries
French bread	
Red wine	
Eggs	
Bacon	
Jelly	
Biscuits	
Orange juice	
Toilet paper	
Toothpaste	
Soap	
Contact solution	
Razor blades	

includes every item that must be purchased is not an external mnemonic. However, if the list contains cues rather than specific items, then the list is a mnemonic. Consider the grocery list in the first column of Table 2.1. This list contains all items needed from a hypothetical trip to the grocery store and is thus not a mnemonic. It is not a mnemonic because it does not aid memory—it simply replaces the need to remember. On the other hand, the list in the second column of Table 2.1 is an external mnemonic because it is composed of a set of cues designed to aid the retrieval of all items to be purchased. This particular external mnemonic uses a categorical organization to condense the grocery list into a smaller more manageable list. Notice that this mnemonic is designed to cue memory for list items by priming the categories of items represented in the list. As such, this type of mnemonic may be subject to recall intrusions. Indeed, the category label "breakfast foods" could lead to the recall of an item such as waffle syrup that did not appear on the original list. This problem is relatively minor considering that, in most cases, it would be worse to forget a needed item than to purchase an item that is not needed immediately.

Mnemonic Properties of List Construction

As mentioned previously, a complete list is not considered a mnemonic if one refers to the list at the time of retrieval. However, research has indicated that construction of a complete list may have mnemonic properties. Intons-Peterson and Fournier (1986) found that preparing a list enhanced memory for to-be-remembered grocery items even when the list was not available at the time of retrieval (see also Barnett, Di Vesta, & Rogozinski, 1981). Apparently, the construction of the list sufficiently enhances encoding to the point that it results in memory improvement. In this case, list construction would be a form of rote rehearsal and would thus be considered a type of internal mnemonic.

In a study somewhat similar to that of Intons-Peterson and Fournier (1986), Brooks, Friedman, and Yesavage (2003) found that instructing older adults to prepare a written list of loci enhanced memory for a list of words despite the fact that participants were not allowed to view their loci list at testing. Although this study involved both internal and external mnemonic factors, it again demonstrates the mnemonic properties of list construction.

Common External Mnemonics

Most external mnemonics are more obviously distinguished from records and internal mnemonics than the examples provided above. The proverbial string tied around a finger is an often mentioned, but rarely used, external mnemonic. More commonly used examples include personal alarms, outlines, pictures, and placing items in locations as cues for remembering. A personal alarm typically involves the sounding of an auditory tone or melody that serves a signal that a task must be completed. Note, however, that successful completion of the task requires that one remembers what course of action is being signified by the tone. One could easily imagine a situation in which a person fails to remember why he set the alarm in the first place. Such a failure corresponds to our previous discussion of prospective memory in which one remembers that something needs to be done but cannot remember what that something is.

Outlines are a type of mnemonic list that provides the learner with a set of topics designed to cue memory for more detailed information subsumed under each topic. Pictures and photographs can also be used to cue memories. Although a photograph of the campsite from a hiking trip provides a permanent record of the site, it can also cue memories about other aspects of the trip that are not directly represented in the picture. The latter function is an example of how pictures can be used as mnemonics. The place method involves leaving an object in a location that will serve as a reminder of an action to be performed. For example, if one needs to remember to return a book to the library, one could leave the book by the door. Notice that the book serves as a cue to remind one to perform the task of returning it to the library. Thus, the to-be-remembered information in this situation is the task to be performed with the book, not the book itself.

Reasons for the Use of External Mnemonics

Interestingly, mnemonic lists and the place method are the memory aids most frequently used by nonpsychologists (Park, Smith, & Cavanaugh, 1990). Moreover, research (Cavanaugh, Grady, & Perlmutter, 1983) suggests that external mnemonics are used more frequently than internal mnemonics. There are several possible reasons for this finding. First, it is likely that the general public is not aware of the variety of effective internal techniques available for improving memory. Even if there is cursory knowledge of the existence of such techniques, it is likely that potential users are unaware of the specific application for which any given mnemonic is designed. As mentioned in Chapter 1, a misapplication of a mnemonic—especially a formal mnemonic—may lead to a general skepticism related to all internal mnemonics.

A second reason that external mnemonics are more frequently used than internal mnemonics may be related to ease of use. In general, the use of external mnemonics reduces cognitive load and provides the learner with a shortcut to remembering. This possibility seems to imply that external mnemonics are more efficient than internal mnemonics. However, this is not necessarily the case. Consider a situation in which a person relies solely on personal alarms and mnemonic lists to aid remembering. The daily demands on memory would require this person to set numerous alarms and manage numerous lists per day. At some point, the management of such lists would itself tax the memory system. Moreover, one could imagine how frequent audible alarms occurring at variable intervals could unnerve friends and coworkers.

Situations Most Amenable to the Use of External Mnemonics

The decision to use an external or internal mnemonic often boils down to personal preference. However, there may be situations in which one or the other type of mnemonic is most appropriate. Intons-Peterson and Fournier (1986) offered six situations in which the use of external mnemonics may be most appropriate:

1. when prospective memory will be tested,
2. when memory is tested after an extremely long retention interval,
3. when the consequences of inaccurate remembering are steep,
4. when to-be-remembered information is especially complicated or otherwise difficult to comprehend,
5. when there is little time for elaboration at encoding, and
6. when memory load is high or attention is divided.

Although we agree that these situations are amenable to the use of external mnemonics, it should be noted that Intons-Peterson and Fournier (1986) constructed their list using an operational definition of external mnemonics different from that used here. Specifically, those authors did not make the distinction between a record of to-be-remembered information and an external mnemonic. They described methods such as writing to-be-remembered information on one's hand as an external mnemonic, whereas we consider such methods to be records of information to be remembered. Nevertheless, Intons-Peterson and Fournier's list of situations for use of external mnemonics fits nicely with the approach taken here.

☐ Self-Generated Versus Other-Generated Mnemonics

A common concern in the selection of a mnemonic is whether learners should choose a preexisting mnemonic devised by someone else or generate the mnemonic themselves. An advantage of using other-generated mnemonics is that there often exists empirical evidence of their effectiveness. Moreover, learners who are unaware of the processes that underlie mnemonic effectiveness may create mnemonics that are limited in effectiveness or completely ineffective. In addition, the creation of mnemonics takes some amount of creativity as well as time and effort. Of course, other-generated mnemonics—especially formal mnemonics—also require time and effort to learn.

A major disadvantage of other-generated mnemonics is that those who use them are often unaware of the specific applications for which a given method is designed. Because the person who constructs a mnemonic is sure to know the purpose for which the mnemonic is constructed, the probability of misapplying an other-generated mnemonic is much higher than the probability of misapplying a self-generated mnemonic. Self-generated mnemonics are also advantageous in that they can be tailored to fit individual learning styles and preferences.

Another major benefit of self-generated mnemonics is that they capitalize on the well-established finding that self-generated information is retained better than provided information (Bobrow & Bower, 1969; Slamecka & Graf, 1978). However, in the context of mnemonics, the effectiveness of self-generated elaboration depends on the complexity of the mnemonic. For example, self-generated elaboration has been demonstrated to be more effective than other-generated elaboration when using simple mnemonics (Ironsmith & Lutz, 1996; Jamieson & Schimpf, 1980; Kuo & Hooper, 2004) but not for mnemonics that are difficult to use (Patton, D'Agaro, & Gaudette, 1991). These findings highlight the distinction between self- and other-generated elaboration and self- and other-generated mnemonics. Self-generated mnemonics will obviously incorporate self-generated elaboration, but other-generated mnemonics may rely on self- or other-generated elaboration. Consider the case of the keyword method that is often used to enhance second-language acquisition. This formal method involves forming a mental image between the meaning of the foreign word and a word from the known language that sounds like the foreign word. For example, in an attempt to learn that the Spanish word *tiesto* means "flowerpot," an English speaker must form an image that combines a flowerpot with an object represented by an English word that sounds similar to the Spanish word *tiesto*. In this case, a proponent of the keyword method might suggest that the English word *tea* be used to form an image of a tea bush growing in a flowerpot. Alternatively, learners may choose to generate their own English words for use with this mnemonic. For instance, a learner might use the English word *test* to form an image of a multiple-choice test on the topic of flowerpots.

As will be evident throughout this book, we believe that knowledge of the processes that underlie effective mnemonics is crucial to selecting an appropriate mnemonic for a given learning situation. Moreover, knowledge of mnemonic processes will allow learners to create mnemonics that are well suited to their personal learning style and to use such self-generated mnemonics with confidence.

☐ Self-Imposed Versus Externally Imposed Mnemonics

An issue related to self-generated versus other-generated mnemonics is whether a mnemonic is self imposed or other imposed. Whereas a self versus other generation deals with who constructs the mnemonic, self versus other imposition deals with who instigates its use. The difference between intentional and incidental learning is at the heart of the issue of self-imposed versus externally imposed mnemonics. Intentional learning involves a conscious effort to commit information to memory. On the other hand, incidental learning occurs without intention to learn or without knowledge of an impending memory test. When a student uses a mnemonic to enhance memory for information that will appear on a test, he is using a self-imposed mnemonic. However, there are occasions in which mnemonics are externally imposed. For example, a professor who uses humorous examples to illustrate important concepts is essentially presenting information in a way that is likely to enhance memory even if the students are not explicitly attempting to memorize the information during the lecture. This type of externally imposed mnemonic can potentially lead to incidental learning, which results in strong test performance even among students who do not study. An intuitive conclusion based on this notion is that educators should most certainly present information to students using mnemonically effective methods. Although we strongly agree with this conclusion, we also acknowledge that individual differences (e.g., personality differences) may moderate the effectiveness of any given externally imposed mnemonic. Thus, to assist as many students as possible, we recommend the use a variety of mnemonic methods in the classroom. The use of mnemonics in education will be discussed further in Chapter 7.

☐ Summary

There are numerous factors that must be considered when selecting a mnemonic for a given learning situation. The type of memory being tested, the nature of the test, and individual differences in ability and style can each influence the effectiveness of a mnemonic. Thus, it is important to know the purpose for which a given mnemonic is designed and keep in mind the goals of the learning situation when choosing a mnemonic. Furthermore, learners should select mnemonics that fit with their individual learning style. These factors should be considered regardless of whether one wishes to use a self-generated or other-generated mnemonic.

Basic Cognitive and Mnemonic Processes

At the heart of the mnemonological approach is the assumption that successful mnemonic techniques tap important basic memory processes, and in that sense, the artificial memory of mnemonics and the natural memory of basic cognitive processes are inherently symbiotic. However obvious this assumption may be, explicit recognition of this relationship between mnemonics and basic processes is important for three reasons. Most important, the mnemonological approach makes explicit that understanding basic memory processes allows for creative development of mnemonic devices, and likewise, any particular mnemonic that has demonstrable effectiveness offers a window into the basic processes. In that sense, basic research and its application have a healthy symbiotic relationship. A less tangible asset of the mnemonological approach is the possible elimination of the tension between natural and artificial learning and memory. Everything relies on the natural memory processes, including the artificial techniques, and for that reason these techniques logically are not artificial. In this chapter, we first discuss basic cognitive processes, which we shall see are identifiable in established mnemonic devices. We then go on to identify additional processes that are common to many mnemonic techniques, indicating that these processes are also potentially important targets for basic memory theory.

☐ Basic Cognitive Processes

Encoding

The initial processing and transformation of information into a mental representation is known as *encoding*. Because encoding is the first step in the active learning process, this process is especially important in determining the success of a mnemonic. The emphasis on basic encoding processes is central to understanding effective mnemonics because the majority of internal mnemonics is designed to facilitate encoding of to-be-remembered information in such a way that allows the information to be successfully stored and retrieved from memory. With this in mind, it is important to note that encoding, storage,[3] and retrieval are highly interdependent processes. Information that is not encoded properly will be difficult (if not impossible) to store and retrieve. Similarly, even if to-be-remembered information is encoded well, it will not be remembered if it is stored in such a way that hinders accurate retrieval. In turn, properly encoded and stored information will not be remembered unless it is successfully retrieved. Thus, because encoding necessarily precedes storage and retrieval, the success of the latter processes depends on the former process. Furthermore, it may very well be the case that the benefits of proper encoding are realized at retrieval. For example, a particular mnemonic technique may involve procedures that lead to the encoding of highly diagnostic retrieval cues. As a result, the mnemonic benefit results from encoding of cues whose ultimate effect is to facilitate retrieval (cf. Tulving, 1983).

Selective Encoding. Hunt (2008) suggested that encoding processes may influence memory in three ways. First, encoding may function to direct attention such that only a select portion of the to-be-remembered information is represented in memory. A good deal of research from the levels-of-processing approach to memory (Craik & Lockhart, 1972) suggests that successful memory depends on orientation toward specific features of to-be-remembered information. For example, Craik and Tulving (1975) presented participants with a list of words with instructions to determine whether each was typed in uppercase or lowercase, whether each word rhymed with a presented word, or whether each word fit meaningfully into a provided sentence frame. The results indicated that the latter condition led to better memory for target words than either of the former conditions. This outcome indicates that orientation toward semantic features leads to better memory than orientation toward superficial features of to-be-remembered information. Extended to mnemonics, these results suggest that to achieve maximal effectiveness, a mnemonic technique must encourage orientation toward meaning rather than the perceptual features of to-be-remembered information.

An important caveat to this conclusion is that the effectiveness of any encoding process is completely dependent on the nature of the memory test. Although orientation to meaning usually yields the best memory, it is also true that most demands on memory are oriented to meaning. If the memory test probes perceptual aspects of the prior experience, perceptual encoding will produce better performance. In basic research, this qualification is represented by the transition from levels of processing to transfer-appropriate processing. Transfer-appropriate processing is the simple principle stating that performance will be best when the demands of the test require the same processes as those engaged by earlier acquisition (Blaxton, 1989; Jacoby, 1983; Morris, Bransford, & Franks, 1977). Successful application of this principle requires that one know the nature of the test demands, something that is rarely possible in most of our daily experiences. Who knows what the world will want to know in the future about most of our mundane activities? However, situations that encourage the use of mnemonics are different. The very fact that we intentionally employ encoding strategies indicates that we know what needs to be remembered. These situations are perfect venues for the application of transfer-appropriate processing.

Transformational Encoding. Encoding may also function to transform the to-be-remembered information such that the resulting mental representation is qualitatively different from the original stimulus. Of course, by definition, a mental representation does not capture stimulus input isomorphically. Thus, when we speak of "transformation," we refer to a gross alteration of stimulus input such as the transformation of a lengthy and complex statement into a simple concept. For example, consider a situation in which a student is presented with Thorndike's (1911) Law of Effect:

> Of several responses made to the same situation, those which are accompanied or closely followed by satisfaction to the animal will, other things being equal, be more firmly connected with the situation, so that, when it recurs, they will be more likely to recur; those which are accompanied or closely followed by discomfort to the animal will, other things being equal, have their connections with that situation weakened, so that, when it recurs, they will be less likely to occur. The greater the satisfaction or discomfort, the greater the strengthening or weakening of the bond. (p. 244)

Given the length and relative complexity of the wording, it is almost certain that the student will not store this statement verbatim in memory. It is more likely that the statement will be encoded in such a way that the gist of the statement is maintained, but the exact wording and the details irrelevant to the student are discarded. For example, the resulting mental representation of the Law of Effect might be something like, "If you do something that leads to a good outcome, you will do it again in a similar situation and vice versa." In this case, the original stimulus input was transformed at encoding such that a succinct interpretation of the original lengthy statement was stored in memory. Another example of transformation encoding would be a guitar player who, upon hearing a series of notes, recognizes the pattern as the pentatonic scale and thus represents it as such in memory. Notice that the original input was individual musical notes but that the encoding was an abstract musical concept. Thus, the notes were transformed from discrete units to a singular pattern and from being auditory to being semantic in nature.

Another common basic encoding process that is relevant to mnemonics is the transformation of modality. That is, the representation of the experience may be transformed from the initial sensory form to a different form. Most common is the two-way transformation between visual and verbal forms. A verbal description may be encoded as a visual image just as a picture may be encoded as a verbal experience. Visual imagery is the most studied of these basic encoding transformations, but in principle, all modalities are candidates for such transformations. Importantly, these transformations do not necessitate that the original representation be replaced. Indeed, most theories of the basic process of visual imagery assume that multiple representations of the same event can be stored in memory (Paivio, 1991).

Visual imagery is an obvious interface between basic concerns with transformational processes at encoding and mnemonic devices because of the prominence of imagery in mnemonics. Transformational encoding is also an essential component of several mnemonic techniques. The use of acronyms involves transformation at encoding such that the to-be-remembered information is reduced to a smaller unit. For example, the acronym "KISS" can be used to remember the mantra of both the computer programmer and the life coach: "Keep it simple, Stupid!" The major system mnemonic also uses transformational encoding. As mentioned in Chapter 1, the major system involves converting large numbers to letters to aid memory. Thus, the conversion from letters to numbers is a transformation that occurs during encoding.

Elaborative Encoding. Elaboration is perhaps the most common function of encoding in the context of mnemonics. Elaboration is the process of embellishing to-be-remembered information with additional features. For example, the formation of mental images to embellish verbal learning material would be considered imaginal elaboration. Similarly, the peg-word method uses elaborative encoding such that to-be-remembered information is associated with a previously learned list of peg words using interactive mental imagery. In this case, the to-be-remembered information is embellished by both association with the peg words and mental imagery.

It should also be noted that the three encoding functions described above are not mutually exclusive. Mnemonics often capitalize on more than one encoding process to enhance memory. For example, the keyword method uses interactive mental imagery to form an association between the translation of a foreign word and what it sounds like when pronounced. Thus, this mnemonic involves selective orientation toward both semantic and phonemic features and elaboration of to-be-remembered information using mental imagery. Similarly, elaboration can be combined with transformational encoding when using acronyms. For example, as acronyms have been found to be more effective when combined with mental imagery, one might imagine the band KISS—a glitzy band renowned for playing simple rock songs—to assist in remembering the "Keep it simple, Stupid" mantra.

Storage

The concept of storage implies that encoded memories are held somewhere. This simple notion that memories are stored is part and parcel of the dominant frameworks for memory, as well as of most people's intuitions about how memory works. The assumption is that different kinds of memories are held in different memory stores. Each storage system has it own characteristics, which include the type of representation that can be stored, the temporal characteristics of the traces in that system, and the memory processes that operate in the formation and use of these traces (Schacter & Tulving, 1994). For example, Atkinson and Shiffrin (1968) described three storage locations: sensory store, short-term store, and long-term store. Information from the environment enters sensory store, which contains only the sensory representation of the original physical energy. If the attention process is allocated to the information, it will be transferred to short-term store. Short-term store is thought to be a temporary storage location with a very limited capacity and originally was assumed to contain only phonetic representations (sound patterns). The process of rehearsal operates within the short-term store, allowing maintenance of the short-lived trace as well as transfer to long-term store. The trace in long-term store enjoyed the temporal characteristic of permanence and was originally assumed to be stored as meaning. Research provoked by the Atkinson and Shiffrin theory resulted in revisions to particular parameters of the framework, but the basic approach to descriptions of memory remains in place and has been extended to include separate systems within both short- and long-term memory (Baddeley, 2000; Schacter, Wagner, & Buckner, 2000).

A particularly influential memory model that does not appeal to separate storage locations is Craik and Lockhart's (1972) levels of processing theory. This theory suggests that quality of processing—not a storage location—determines the permanence of to-be-remembered information in memory. From this perspective, the storage process is, for the most part, irrelevant. Rather, emphasis is placed on the type of encoding and whether the encoding conditions match the conditions of retrieval. The latter notion is the essence of Morris et al.'s (1977) principle of transfer-appropriate processing. In a nutshell, this principle states that the features selected for encoding must correspond to the nature of the memory test for successful recovery of learned information. That is, if the memory test emphasizes the meaning of to-be-remembered information, then successful memory will require encoding of meaning. As such, the principle of transfer-appropriate processing implies an interdependence between encoding and retrieval—a notion that is further reinforced by the encoding specificity principle (Thomson & Tulving, 1970; Tulving & Thomson, 1973). The encoding specificity principle simply states that successful retrieval depends on the retrieval cue being present at the time of encoding. Thus, from a levels of processing approach, successful memory can be explained solely in terms of encoding and retrieval without appealing to storage.

Although the storage concept is not necessary to explain mnemonic functioning, it is worth noting that the structure of information in memory may have some bearing on mnemonic success. For example, it is widely believed that learned information is represented in memory in a way that is highly organized even when that information is not originally presented in an organized fashion (Bousefield, 1953) or if the information is ostensibly unrelated (Tulving, 1962). The implication of these findings is that mnemonics that serve to organize to-be-remembered information may enhance memory by arranging the information in a way that matches the organization of preexisting knowledge. That is, organization allows the to-be-remembered information to be more efficiently accommodated by preexisting knowledge structures. One could interpret this to mean that organization makes storage more efficient. However, an equally plausible interpretation from the perspective of transfer-appropriate processing is that organizational processing facilitates later performance if the test overlaps with those organizational processing demands.

Retrieval

Retrieval is the process of recovering information from memory. As noted earlier, the retrieval of information is highly dependent on the nature of the encoding process. Successful retrieval can occur only when the conditions of encoding match the conditions of retrieval (transfer-appropriate processing) and if the cue being used to access learned information was present at the time of encoding (encoding specificity). From this perspective, retrieval is simply a process of using cues to narrow the set of possible responses until only target information remains to be recovered or until the set of possible responses is exhausted without successful recovery of the target. Thus, mnemonic success will depend on the extent to which a given technique encourages encoding of cues that are useful at the time of retrieval. Cues that uniquely identify specific learned information will be more effective than cues that provide access to more general aspects of the target information.

The importance of uniquely identifying cues is made salient when one considers the potential influence of interfering information at retrieval. Interference occurs when either newly learned information makes retrieval of previously learned information more difficult (retroactive interference) or when previously learned information makes the retrieval of newly learned information more difficult (proactive interference). The extent to which additional learning interferes with the retrieval of target information depends on the similarity between the interfering information and the target information. Specifically, information that is highly similar to target information is more likely to cause interference than is dissimilar information (McGeoch & McDonald, 1931). Thus, uniquely identifying cues that are highly diagnostic of the target information will be more resistant to interference than more general cues. The notion of cue diagnosticity is important in the context of mnemonics because many mnemonics involve procedures that function to provide cues that will make the to-be-remembered information highly discriminable at retrieval. For example, mnemonic procedures that incorporate elaborative encoding in order to enhance distinctive processing of to-be-remembered information are believed to be successful in part because they result in highly effective retrieval cues (Hunt & McDaniel, 1993; Hunt & Smith, 1996; McDaniel, DeLosh, & Merritt, 2000; Waddill & McDaniel, 1998).

Memory tests differ in the kind of cue information available at the time of retrieval. So-called free recall tests are often characterized as providing no cues, but this is an overstatement in that the free recall situation always is accompanied by cues. These cues, however, are general and low in diagnosticity for particular items. For example, a question such as "What did you do in Chicago?" is analogous to the laboratory instruction to "recall all of the items that I showed you." In both cases, there is useful cue information as contrasted with the request "What did you do?" but this information circumscribes a general event from which the specific items must be generated. Cued recall tests offer more diagnostic information in that the cue specifies a particular event or item of interest. For example, the cue information in the request "What was your favorite piece at the Art Institute in Chicago?" is much more specific than "What did you do in Chicago?" Even more supportive is the cue information in a recognition test where one is required to decide whether an item was or was not part of a specified prior experience. Recognition does not require the generation of the item itself, but it does demand discriminative decisions about particular past experiences.

The different cue environments impose different demands on psychological processes at the time of retrieval. Consequently it is not surprising that the effectiveness of mnemonic techniques varies as a function of the type of memory test. For example, compared to standard verbal encoding, performance encoding leads to greater memory improvement in recognition than in free recall (Mohr, Engelkamp, & Zimmer, 1989). Similarly, when learners were tested after short retention intervals, bizarre imagery typically improved free recall but not cued recall (Wollen & Cox, 1981). These findings suggest that certain mnemonics may enhance memory mainly by enhancing discriminability of target information, whereas others may serve mainly to facilitate the generative aspects of retrieval.

☐ Specific Encoding Processes Fundamental to Mnemonic Success

Organization

Organization is the process of grouping individual items based on shared relationships among differing items. For example, a list such as *Audrey, Andrew, Carla, Floyd, Rita, Hugo, Katrina,* and *Ivan* could be organized based on several different relationships among items. Perhaps the most common organization would be to group the list into a set of women's names (*Audrey, Carla, Rita,* and *Katrina*) and a set of men's names (*Andrew, Floyd, Hugo,* and *Ivan*). However, a meteorologist might organize the same list under a single category: retired hurricane names. A third possible organization would be to group the list into a set of names that end in vowels and a set of names that end in consonants. In all three examples, list items are grouped based on shared features that could be cued by a category label. Thus, organization is simply the encoding of similarities among items—a process that is referred to as *relational processing.*

Although a good deal of research (e.g., Bower, Clark, Lesgold, & Winzenz, 1969; Cohen, 1963) suggests that organized information is easier to remember than unorganized information, other research indicates that relational processing alone has limited mnemonic effectiveness. For example, Tulving and Pearlstone (1966) presented participants with lists organized by categories. Each list contained category labels and a number of items from each category. The presentation of the list was such that items from a given category immediately followed the category label. After list presentation, participants were given a free recall test followed by a cued recall test. The results indicated that recall cued by category labels increased the number of categories for which at least one item was recalled (category access) relative to free recall. However, the number of items recalled within each category did not differ as a function of the type of recall test. An identical pattern of results was found in a study (Lewis, 1971) in which category labels were not included in the presented lists. These findings suggest that relational processing enhances access to general categories of learned information, but it does not aid in the discrimination of individual target items composing the category. Moreover, this research suggests that mnemonic techniques that rely solely on relational processing (i.e., categorical and schematic mnemonics) are likely to be limited in their effectiveness. In keeping with this notion, the most effective mnemonics include procedures that engage relational processing, but they do not rely on it as the sole mechanism for effectiveness.

Elaboration

In many ways, elaboration serves a function opposite to that of organization. Whereas organizational processing focuses on the relations among to-be-remembered information, elaboration functions to embellish the meaning of individual items. The effect of elaborative processing is to make the items more discriminable by producing uniquely identifying cues that distinguish the to-be-remembered information from competing information. Thus, whereas organization involves processing of similarities (relational processing), elaboration involves processing of differences. The specific types of differences that are processed are those that are uniquely specific to each to-be-remembered item. This type of processing is commonly referred to as *item-specific processing*. The importance of item-specific processing is that it encourages encoding that results in highly diagnostic retrieval cues.

As mentioned earlier, elaboration is a common component of mnemonic techniques. However, for any given mnemonic, elaboration can be either meaningful or nonmeaningful. We describe these two different types of elaboration below.

Meaningful Elaboration. Craik and Tulving's (1975) finding of better memory when participants determined whether target words fit into a sentence frame compared to when they determined the case or phonology of the words suggests that elaboration of word meaning enhances memory. In a similar study, Bradshaw and Anderson (1982) presented participants with facts of historical figures that were followed by either elaboration with related facts, elaboration with unrelated facts, or no elaboration at all. The results of their Experiment 3 indicated that facts that had received related elaboration were remembered better than facts that had received unrelated or no elaboration. Consistent with these results, Kerr and Winograd (1982) found that facial recognition was enhanced by the addition of descriptive phrases of the target person at encoding. These findings indicate that the processing of meaning in the form of relevant thematically related information also enhances memory. In the context of mnemonics, these results suggest that procedures that encourage the learner to consider non-essential but related facts that expand upon the gist of the to-be-remembered information can be beneficial. For example, a teacher might make learning material more memorable by simply supplementing the standard information with several real-world examples.

A slightly different type of meaningful elaboration that can be effective for enhancing memory was demonstrated by Rogers, Kuiper, and Kirker (1977). In their Experiment 1, participants were presented with a list of trait adjectives with instructions to determine either whether each adjective was typed in small or large letters, whether each adjective rhymed with a provided word, whether each adjective meant the same as a provided word, or whether each adjective described themselves. The results indicated that free recall in the self-referencing condition led to more recall than in the semantic condition and that both the semantic and the self-referencing conditions resulted in better memory than the other two conditions. These results suggest that considering information in relation to the self—perhaps the most well-established concept in memory—is an especially powerful form of elaboration. In keeping with this notion, other researchers (e.g., Hyde & Jenkins, 1969; Packman & Battig, 1978) have also found that judgments that involve subjective evaluations that presumably involve self-referencing (i.e., pleasantness) increase memory relative to judgments based on objective or superficial features (Hyde & Jenkins, 1973; Packman & Battig, 1978). Related specifically to mnemonics, these findings suggest that procedures that encourage subjective appraisal should strongly enhance recall. For example, when presented with new information, one could simply ask oneself a series of questions such as "Do I agree with this idea? Do I like the implications of this? Does this information fit with what I already know?" Based on the research described above, simply asking these questions should result in strong memory for the new information.

Nonmeaningful Elaboration. Although research clearly supports the idea that meaningful elaboration enhances memory, some research suggests that it is more extensive processing, not necessarily more meaningful processing, that facilitates memory. For example, Kolers and Perkins (1975) demonstrated better memory for sentences that were presented to participants in an upside-down fashion than if the sentences were presented normally (see also Graf, 1982). On the basis of such findings, Kolers (1979) argued that the upside-down sentences require additional processing, which accounts for the memory advantage. Notice that, in this case, the additional processing referred to by Kolers did not involve meaningful elaboration. Thus, it appears that elaborative processing can enhance memory even if it is not meaningful.

Research on the generation effect—better memory for information that is self-generated than for information that is provided—also supports the notion that nonmeaningful elaboration can enhance memory. Slamecka and Graf (1978) had participants either read synonym or rhyming word pairs or generate words that either shared the same meaning or rhymed with a presented word. In keeping with the notion that meaningful elaboration facilitates memory, recognition of synonyms exceeded that of rhymes. However, generation of rhymes also led to better memory than simply reading. Thus, it appears that both meaningful and nonmeaningful elaboration can enhance memory.

Distinctive Processing

As discussed, both relational processing (i.e., organization) and item-specific processing (i.e., elaboration) appear to enhance memory. As pointed out by previous researchers (e.g., Hunt, 2006; Hunt & McDaniel, 1993), these findings can, on the surface, seem a bit puzzling. That is, how can it be that both processing differences and processing similarities lead to better memory? The answer lies with the well-established finding that distinctiveness facilitates memory.

Hunt (2006) defined distinctiveness as "the processing of difference in the context of similarity" (p. 11). Essentially, this means that distinctiveness results from a combination of item-specific and relational processing. Previous research (e.g., Einstein & Hunt, 1980; Hunt & Einstein, 1981) has demonstrated that both item-specific and relational processing facilitate memory but that memory is maximized when the two processing types occur together. For example, Einstein and Hunt presented participants with lists of words that could be grouped into either obvious or nonobvious categories. Participants receiving each type of list either rated the pleasantness of each word on the list or sorted the words into categories. The results indicated that with lists representing obvious categories, pleasantness rating led to better memory than sorting. However, the opposite was true with lists representing less obvious categories. Assuming that the lists representing obvious categories encouraged more relational processing than lists that were less amenable to categorization and that the pleasantness-rating task encouraged more item-specific processing than the sorting task, the results suggest that the combination of item-specific and relational processing leads to better memory than either type of processing alone.

How do item-specific and relational processing work together to aid memory? Hunt (2006) suggested that relational processing serves to delimit our search for to-be-remembered items at the time of retrieval. For example, when learners are presented with a list of names of North American mammals, the similarity shared among list items allows learners to recall the general class of information that must be remembered: animal names. However, the ability to recover specific items from the list will depend not on similarities among learned items but on uniquely identifying features. Thus, the precise specification of items to be remembered within the category necessitates the processing of item-specific features. Using the example from above, a hunter might remember that deer, squirrel, and boar were on the list because those items differed from the other items by virtue of them being animals that he has hunted (cf. Van Overschelde, Rawson, Dunlosky, & Hunt, 2005). Taken together, this means that relational information provides a general frame of reference for what type of information must be remembered, and item-specific information allows one to discriminate between items that were and were not on the list.

Extended to mnemonics, research on distinctiveness and memory suggests that a combination of item-specific and relational processing is necessary for maximal memory performance. Thus, mnemonic techniques that serve to organize and embellish to-be-remembered information will be more effective than techniques that function only to organize or only to embellish. Moreover, this also suggests that purely organizational mnemonics can be made more effective by adding procedures that encourage item-specific processing. Similarly, the addition of procedures that encourage relational processing to purely elaborative mnemonics should also increase effectiveness.

It should, however, be noted that even when a combination of item-specific and relational processing is used, too much item-specific processing can result in effects detrimental to memory. For example, Worthen and Loveland (2003) found that bizarreness increased the ratio of disruptive to facilitative effects in memory for self-performed acts compared to other-performed acts. Given that both bizarreness (Wollen & Margres, 1987) and self-performance (Engelkamp, 1995; Engelkamp & Dehn, 2000) are thought to elicit spontaneous item-specific processing, the authors concluded that the item-specific processing induced by both variables led to an excess of item-specific processing, which ultimately resulted in poor binding of the elements composing the event (cf. Craik, 2006). Thus, some degree of balance between item-specific and relational processing should be sought when combining different mnemonic procedures.

Mental Imagery

As discussed in Chapter 1, the use of mental imagery to facilitate memory has a long and storied history. Although visual mental imagery is the most common form of imagery used in mnemonics, mental imagery can be produced for any of the senses. Below we discuss the three types of imagery that have received the most attention from memory researchers.

Visual Mental Imagery. A good deal of research (e.g., Bower, 1970b; May & Clayton, 1973; Paivio, 1969; Richardson, 1978) suggests that visual mental imagery enhances memory. Typically, instructions to form *interactive* mental images lead to the greatest mnemonic advantage (Bower, 1970a; Epstein, Rock, & Zuckerman, 1960). An interactive mental image is one in which the components of a particular to-be-remembered item are combined in a single image. For example, in a paired-associate learning task, one of the to-be-remembered target pairs might be *table–lamp*. In this case, imagining a lamp sitting on a table would result in better memory than imagining the two items separately.

According to Paivio (1991), mental imagery enhances memory by providing an additional cue to aid retrieval. That is, if to-be-remembered verbal information is also imagined, then the target information is encoded both verbally and imaginally. At retrieval, either cue could be used to recover the target information. On the other hand, verbal information that is not encoded imaginally (only verbally) will, with all else being equal, have only one cue to aid retrieval. Thus, the beneficial effects of imagery on memory are the result of the additional cue provided by imaginal encoding.

An alternative view of the influence of imagery on memory is provided by Hunt and Marschark (1987). These authors suggested that mental imagery facilitates memory because it encourages distinctive processing. Specifically, they argued that imagery provides item-specific information that, when combined with relational information, results in better memory. In support of their view, Marschark and Hunt (1989) demonstrated that the beneficial effects of mental imagery can be attenuated or eliminated altogether under conditions that discourage relational processing.

Although the distinctive-processing view emphasizes item-specific information provided by mental imagery, that is not to say that imagery is purely elaborative. As noted by Hunt and Marschark (1987), the extent to which imagery serves an elaborative or organizational function depends on whether the imagery is applied to an entire event or to an item within an event. For example, if separate interactive mental images are formed for each pair in a list of 10 word pairs, then the images will serve a mainly elaborative function that enhances the discriminability of each to-be-remembered pair. However, if a single interactive image including all items from the list is used to reduce the list items into a single meaningful unit, then the imagery will also serve an organizational function. Thus, the extent to which mental imagery provides item-specific, relational, or both types of information will depend on how the imagery is applied to the to-be-remembered information.

An important consideration when using visual mental imagery is whether common or bizarre mental imagery should be used. As discussed in Chapter 1, the use of bizarre mental imagery to enhance memory has been advocated for thousands of years. However, existing empirical research on the effectiveness of bizarre imagery as a mnemonic suggests that there are limits to its effectiveness. First, bizarre imagery leads to better memory than does common imagery only when both types of imagery are used within the same list. Thus, the bizarreness advantage occurs when some list items are learned using bizarre imagery and other items are learned with common imagery, but not when bizarre imagery is applied to the entire list (McDaniel et al., 2000; McDaniel & Einstein, 1986; McDaniel, Einstein, DeLosh, May, & Brady, 1995). Perhaps even more revealing is the finding that when both imagery types are used in the same list, memory for information encoded with bizarre imagery is remembered at the expense of items encoded with common imagery (Kroll & Tu, 1988; Lang, 1995). This suggests that bizarre imagery does not increase the total number of items remembered but simply allows the learner to select which list items will have the highest probability of being recalled. It should be noted, however, that an exception to the bizarre–common trade-off has been found when the majority, but not all, of a list is encoded using common imagery. That is, the use of a few bizarre encodings and many common encodings has, on occasion, been found to increase the overall number of list items remembered (see Worthen, 2006, for a discussion).

Another problem associated with the use of bizarre imagery as a mnemonic is that bizarre elaboration enhances access of target events from memory, but it does not increase the amount of detail recovered. For example, research on memory for sentences (e.g., Burns, 1996; Kroll & Tu, 1988; McDaniel & Einstein, 1986; Worthen, Garcia-Rivas, Green, & Vidos, 2000) has demonstrated that although more bizarre than common sentences are accessed (at least one word recalled), the number of words recalled per sentence is greater for common than bizarre items. This finding in combination with the limitations described suggests that bizarre imagery may not be particularly effective as a stand-alone mnemonic.

Despite the potential limitations of using bizarre imagery as the sole mechanism for mnemonic functioning, bizarre imagery can be effective as a component of a mnemonic system. For example, Worthen, Fontenelle, Deschamps, and Foreman (2008) examined the role of common and bizarre imagery in determining the effectiveness of the keyword mnemonic as a method to learn Spanish vocabulary. The results indicated that the keyword method led to the recall of more correct definitions than a control condition but only when common imagery or both bizarre and common imagery was used. These results suggest that in the context of the keyword mnemonic, bizarreness does not impair memory for details and is at least as effective as common imagery. The latter point is important because it is sometimes difficult to create common images while using the keyword method.

There is little doubt that bizarre imagery provides item-specific information that has the potential to aid retrieval. However, the relative effectiveness of bizarre imagery may depend on the extent to which relational information is also available at the time of encoding. Without relational information, bizarre imagery is likely to result in poorly integrated memories. However, when combined with relational processing, the problems associated with bizarre imagery will be diminished. Thus, the use of bizarre imagery as a component of a mnemonic system must be complemented by procedures that encourage relational processing for maximal mnemonic effectiveness.

Kinesthetic Imagery. Kinesthetic imagery involves imagining oneself performing a motor action while focusing on muscle positions and physical movements. This is not to be confused with kinesthetic practice, which involves performing the motor movements involved with a particular action without actually performing the task. To clarify the distinction, consider a situation in which one wishes to increase shot accuracy in archery. If one imagined oneself using correct form to draw the bow and release the arrow, then one would be using kinesthetic imagery. However, if one practiced the movements associated with correct form in the absence of the bow, this would be kinesthetic practice. Of course, if one simply took additional shots with the bow using correct form under controlled conditions, this would be considered standard physical practice.

Empirical research on the effects of kinesthetic imagery on memory is almost exclusively focused on procedural memory. For example, research has shown that kinesthetic imagery can enhance free throw shooting in basketball. Clark (1960) found that for experienced players, kinesthetic imagery enhanced free throw shooting ability almost to the same extent as physical practice. However, for less experienced players, physical practice was significantly more effective than imagery. Extending this finding, Ziegler (1987) demonstrated that a combination of kinesthetic practice and kinesthetic imagery enhanced free throw shooting performance more than imagery alone or standard practice alone. This result has also been found in studies examining skills such as figure skating (Mumford & Hall, 1985), karate (Ryan, Blakeslee, & Furst, 1986), and swimming (White, Ashton, & Lewis, 1979). However, across research domains, the general pattern of results is that mental practice increases performance compared to no practice at all, but that standard physical practice leads to the best performance (Murphy, 1990).

Auditory Imagery. Auditory mental imagery involves imagining an auditory experience (e.g., a sound or sounds) in the absence of corresponding auditory input (cf. Intons-Peterson, 1992). Only a scant amount of research has been conducted in the area of auditory imagery, and even less has focused on its relationship with memory. Previous research suggests that auditory imagery reproduces many of the facets of auditory sensory experiences. For example, research has demonstrated that auditory imagery contains information about pitch (Farah & Smith, 1983), loudness (Intons-Peterson, 1992), and timbre (Crowder, 1989). More relevant to the topic of mnemonics, previous research has produced some evidence that suggests auditory imagery facilitates memory in ways similar to visual and kinesthetic imagery. For example, Tinti, Cornoldi, and Marschark (1997) found that interactive auditory imagery resulted in better memory than noninteracting auditory imagery (Experiment 1) and that interactive auditory imagery enhanced memory better than verbal elaboration (Experiment 3). However, research by Winnick and Brody (1984) suggests that the facilitative effects of auditory imagery may be moderated by the imagery value of to-be-remembered information. Specifically, Winnick and Brody presented participants with words that were low in imagery value (e.g., *perjury*), high in visual imagery (e.g., *peach*), high in auditory imagery (e.g., *giggle*), and high in both visual and auditory imagery (e.g., *guitar*). The results indicated that for low-imagery words and auditory imagery words, instructions to form visual or auditory imagery did not enhance memory relative to a control. However, both instructions to form visual imagery and instructions to form auditory imagery enhanced memory for words high in both types of imagery. The same authors also reported results of an additional experiment (Experiment 3), which combined a drawing with visual imagery and vocalization with auditory imagery. Although the interpretation of the results is complicated by the lack of a control group, inspection of the means between experiments suggests that the addition of the quasi-kinesthetic practice enhanced memory more than imagery alone.

□ Summary

Regardless of one's theoretical approach to memory, there is general agreement that encoding and retrieval are interdependent processes. Although the concept of storage is not necessary from our perspective, it can also be safely assumed that encoding, storage, and retrieval are interdependent. Regardless, it is clear that factors that influence encoding will ultimately affect retrieval. Without proper encoding, information will not be remembered. Although encoding can proceed in a variety of ways, the crucial factor is whether encoding encourages item-specific processing, relational processing, or both. Encoding procedures that encourage relational processing will result in successful access of the general frame of reference that contains the type of information that must be remembered. Encoding procedures that encourage item-specific processing will make the to-be-remembered information more discriminable. It then follows that accurate discrimination of target items within a specified context requires a combination of item-specific and relational processing. In terms of creating successful mnemonics, this means that any given mnemonic system should include procedures that encourage both item-specific and relational processing. Specifically how these types of processing can be induced can vary. However, in a general sense, relational processing will be induced by procedures that encourage organization of to-be-remembered information, and item-specific processing will be induced by elaboration. Because a combination of item-specific and relational processing is crucial for successful mnemonic functioning, the assessment of the potential success of a given mnemonic requires an ability to identify procedures that encourage each type of processing. This is the essence of mnemonology: examining mnemonics in terms of their underlying processes to understand their strengths and weaknesses. In the following two chapters, we examine existing mnemonics from a mnemonological approach.

Formal Mnemonic Systems

Formal mnemonics are those that involve highly prescribed instructions for use. Whereas a simple mnemonic procedure such as semantic elaboration puts very few constraints on the learner, formal mnemonics provide a more precise specification of how information should be encoded and retrieved. In most cases, a learner using a formal mnemonic is applying a technique that has been developed by someone else. As discussed in Chapter 2, this type of learning situation has advantages and disadvantages. One advantage of using a preexisting formal technique is that there is usually some evidence—even if anecdotal—that attests to its effectiveness. Second, other-generated techniques relieve one of the burden of creating a mnemonic from scratch. However, these advantages are sometimes offset by a lack of knowledge of the applications for which the mnemonic was designed and the time required to learn the technique. Regardless, the present discussion is offered not to promote the use of formal mnemonic systems but to provide insight into the mechanics of such techniques. By examining the procedures involved in each system in light of basic cognitive processes, we can identify the functional components that underlie each system. Thus, the present chapter will be beneficial both to those who wish to learn and use formal mnemonic systems and to those who wish to devise their own mnemonic techniques. Below, we discuss some of the most widely used and well-researched formal techniques.

☐ Method of Loci

As mentioned in Chapter 1, the method of loci is perhaps the oldest surviving formal mnemonic. The method of loci is an internal mnemonic that can be used to aid recall of ordered topics to be addressed in a long speech. Thus, contrary to popular belief, this method was not specifically designed for simple list learning, and it is not limited to that application.

Basic Procedures. Use of the method of loci begins with the formation of a visual mental image of a very familiar place—preferably one with several sections or rooms. This imagined place will ultimately serve as a foundation for both encoding and retrieval of the to-be-remembered information. Next, a visual mental image of each to-be-remembered item is created and placed in a specific location within the previously imagined familiar place. Placement of items proceeds with the first item being placed near the entry of the imagined place and each succeeding item placed increasingly further toward the interior. When the information needs to be recalled, the learner mentally revisits the familiar place and collects the items that had been placed there. Other than these general instructions, there are few additional constraints on how one can implement the mnemonic. One possible exception is the suggestion that to-be-remembered items should not be hidden within the image of the familiar place. For example, when trying to remember an item such as *milk*, one should not imagine it in a concealed location such as inside a refrigerator. However, the research on memory for concealed mental images has been mixed. Kerr and Neisser (1983; also Neisser & Kerr, 1973) demonstrated that concealed images are just as mnemonically effective as unconcealed images. Others (Iaccino & Byrne, 1989; Keenan & Moore, 1979) have suggested that unconcealed images, with tightly prescribed instructions to conceal, are more mnemonically successful than concealed images. Apparently, the moderating factor underlying the discrepancy between the results is the time required to form images (Keenan, 1983; Kerr & Neisser, 1983). If time to form images is constrained, then concealed imagery leads to poorer recall than unconcealed imagery. However, with ample time for image formation, there should be no difference between the mnemonic effectiveness of concealed and unconcealed images.

Example of Use. There is a variety of ways to apply the instructions for use of the method of loci. As a result, there may be some slight variability in the mnemonic implications associated with different manifestations of the technique. However, the most fundamental procedures of the system rely on the application of a few basic cognitive processes. We will first provide an example of a typical manifestation of the method of loci and then examine the processes that underlie the system.

Consider a situation in which a conservationist will be delivering a speech and wishes to discuss, in order, five famous figures as they relate to wildlife conservation: Aldo Leopold, Saxton Pope and Arthur Young, Theodore Roosevelt, and John Huston. Aldo Leopold was, among other things, a fisherman, a hunter, and a professor of game management at the University of Wisconsin. Often considered the "Father of Wildlife Management," Leopold's posthumously published *A Sand County Almanac*

(1949) is one of the most influential books in the area of ecology. Saxton Pope was a medical doctor and instructor of surgery at the University of California who, along with Arthur Young, set a standard of ethics for traditional bow hunting. The Pope and Young Club created in their honor is a leading conservationist organization that advocates responsible fair-chase hunting. Theodore Roosevelt, the 26th president of the United States, was a staunch conservationist who cofounded the American Bison Society and was instrumental in the establishment of the National Forest Service. John Huston was an actor and legendary film director whose elephant-hunting experience in Africa serves as a cautionary tale for hunters with ignoble intentions. Using aliases, Peter Viertel's (1953) *White Hunter Black Heart*[4] reveals that, while filming *The African Queen* (Eagle, Woolf, & Huston, 1951), Huston became obsessed with killing an elephant even though he thought the act would be sinful. However, when presented with an opportunity to shoot an elephant, Huston had a crisis of conscience. As a result, Huston hesitated in the presence of the elephant, which then charged and killed a hunting guide who had attempted to protect him from the elephant.

The situation described above is perfectly suited for the use of the method of loci. As with classic applications of the method, this example involves remembering specific topics that will be discussed in a particular order. Let us now consider how the method of loci could be applied.

The first step in using the method of loci is to identify a familiar place whose image can be used to organize the topics of the speech. Let us say that the conservationist will use the building in which she works as her familiar place. To remember to discuss Aldo Leopold, she might first transform the name "Leopold" into the phonetically similar "Leo poled." As "Leo" is represented by a lion in both astronomy and astrology, an image of "Leo poled" can be formed by visualizing a lion climbing the flagpole in front of the conservationist's building. To remember Saxton Pope and Arthur Young, the conservationist could form an image of the Pope holding an infant (used to represent "Young") at the front door of the building. An image of Theodore Roosevelt sitting at the receptionist's desk holding a teddy bear (his namesake) could be used to remember the 26th president. Finally, an image of a large map of Houston (a city in Texas whose pronunciation is identical to Huston) posted in front of the elevator door could be used to remember John Huston.

When the conservationist must deliver her speech, she will mentally navigate her office building and "pick up" the cues that she placed there earlier. She will begin at the outside of her building where she will encounter the flagpole, which now should be associated with the image of an ascending lion. The lion represents "Leo" and thus the "Leo poled" image will cue Aldo *Leopold*. Moving closer toward the building, she encounters the Pope holding an infant, which will cue Saxton *Pope* and Arthur *Young*.

Upon entering the building she finds *Theodore* Roosevelt holding a teddy bear at the receptionist's desk, which will, of course, help her remember to discuss this figure. Finally, at the elevator, the conservationist will see a large map of Houston, which will cue the name "Huston" and thus assist in remembering to discuss John *Huston*. Of course, in keeping with the classic use of the method of loci, these procedures will not necessarily assist in remembering the details of the speech. Rather, this application of the method is used to help remember the topics to be discussed in order.

When considering the example provided here, one should note that each image could be further embellished in an effort to improve memory for information that the learner finds especially problematic. For example, if the conservationist finds that she is having trouble remembering the first names of Pope and Young, she could embellish the corresponding image with additional cues such as a saxophone also being held by the Pope and a paintbrush being held by the infant. In this example, the saxophone would be used to cue *Saxton* and the paintbrush would be used to cue *Art* (short for Arthur).

Underlying Processes. In a general sense, this example makes extensive use of elaborative encoding by the association of the to-be-remembered figures with more well-established memories (locations within a familiar place). The use of interactive mental imagery provides another degree of elaboration, which provides additional item-specific information and thus should greatly enhance the discriminability of the target information.

Because the nature of each interactive image varies slightly, it may be important to consider the mnemonic techniques used in the formation of the individual images. The first image involves both transformational and selective encoding. *Aldo Leopold* was transformed into the more easily imaged and phonetically similar *Leo Poled*. The transformation of the name into a phonetic equivalent involves selective encoding because it results from orientation toward phonemic features of the to-be-remembered item. Also, the resulting image is a bizarre interactive image. An image of the Pope holding an infant was used to represent *Saxton Pope* and *Arthur Young*. This image also uses transformational encoding—most obviously in the transformation of *Young* into a concrete interactive image of an infant. The image of Theodore Roosevelt does not involve transformational encoding, but it does involve elaborative encoding by embellishing the image of the former president with a teddy bear. The inclusion of the teddy bear in the image may also be bizarre depending on how it was imaged. Transformational encoding is used when a common image of the map of Houston is used to represent John Huston. It should be noted that some psychologists (e.g., Bower, 1970a) have suggested that the mental images used should be as similar to the to-be-remembered items as possible. However, this is typically not feasible when the to-be-remembered items are abstract or otherwise difficult to image.

Although a good deal of elaboration is involved in the use of the method of loci, organization is also a key component. In our example, the information is organized by placing the information that must be remembered first in exterior locations of the imagined place, and information that is to be remembered later is placed in the interior of the image. This type of placement maintains the serial order of the information such that it can be recalled in proper order. Moreover, the serial organization inherent to the method of loci allows the learner to know how to begin and complete the retrieval process: Retrieval begins at the first location in the familiar image and ends when either all to-be-remembered items have been recovered or all locations have been searched. The use of interactive mental images to associate the to-be-remembered information to the familiar place also serves to consolidate all of the information into a single meaningful unit. The combination of elaborative and organizational techniques used in this example will lead to distinctive processing, which should result in mnemonic effectiveness.

Research Support. Powerful evidence of the effectiveness of the method of loci comes from feats of exceptional memory described in case studies (e.g., Luria, 1968). However, empirical research (e.g., Roediger, 1980) has also demonstrated the method to be effective in enhancing serial recall even after a substantial retention interval (Wang & Thomas, 2000). In addition, research (De Beni & Cornoldi, 1988; Massen & Vaterrodt-Plunnecke, 2006) has found that repeated use of the same loci for different lists does not diminish the effectiveness of the method. However, research with normal populations has shown that self-generated loci are more effective than loci that are supplied by others (see Moe & De Beni, 2004).

There are a few limitations to the effectiveness of the method of loci. For example, Cornoldi and De Beni (1991) and Moe and De Beni (2005) demonstrated the method of loci to be more effective than cumulative verbal rehearsal for learning complicated verbal material (e.g., extensive discourse) with oral but not written presentation. Also, Canellopoulou and Richardson (1998) found that neurologically impaired participants benefit from the method of loci when imagery is provided but not with self-generated imagery. This finding is consistent with the argument that formal mnemonics may be too cumbersome for brain-injured learners (McKinlay, 1992; Richardson, 1995).

☐ The Peg-Word Method

The peg-word method is typically used for serial learning of lists; however, the method could be helpful in any situation that demands accurate serial recall.

Basic Procedures. The first step in using the peg-word method is to learn a list of peg words that will serve as a framework for the organization of to-be-remembered lists. Most commonly, the list of peg words rhymes with numbers. For example, the peg-words list might include the words *bun, shoe, tree, door, hive, sticks, heaven, gate, wine,* and *hen.* Notice that the words in this list rhyme, in serial order, with the numbers 1 through 10. After committing the peg-word list to memory, the learner forms an interactive mental image between each to-be-remembered item and a peg word. Thus, the first image formed will include the first target-list item and the first peg word (*bun*), the second image will include the second target-list item and the second peg word (*shoe*), and so on. At the time of retrieval, the learner begins a serial progression through the numbers 1 through 10, which will cue the peg words and the target items associated with them.

Example of Use. Consider a situation in which a history student must learn details associated with the Antiquities Act of 1906. Formally known as An Act for the Preservation of American Antiquities, this act has been used by U.S. presidents to establish national monuments. In this case, let us say that the history student wishes to use the peg-word method to remember the first five national monuments in the order that they were established. The first national monument established was Devils Tower—a landform created from volcanic activity in what is now Crook County, Wyoming. To remember this monument, the student might form an interactive mental image of a devil eating a bun at the top of a tower. The second national monument established was the Petrified Forest. Located in Apache and Navajo counties, Arizona, the Petrified Forest is one of the largest concentrations of petrified wood in the world. The student might imagine a pair shoes made of petrified wood (e.g., a colorful pair of clogs) to remember this monument. The third national monument to be established was Montezuma Castle in Yavapai County, Arizona. Montezuma Castle is an area of cliff dwellings inhabited by the Sinagua people in the 1400s. This monument could be remembered by forming an image of a castle nestled in a tree like a tree house. If the student wishes to add an additional cue to remember "Montezuma," he could place a large "M" at the entrance of the castle. Inscription Rock (known formally as El Morro) was the fourth national monument established. Inscription Rock is sandstone bluff in Cibola County, New Mexico, on which Native American petroglyphs and inscriptions from early Spanish explorers were carved. The student could remember this monument by forming a mental image of a door made of rock and sandstone that might also include carvings. Located in San Juan and McKinley counties, New Mexico, Chaco Canyon was the fifth national monument established. It contains a large concentration of ruins of the ancient Pueblo people who inhabited the area between 900 and 1150 (AD). To remember this monument, the student could imagine a beehive in a canyon that is swarming with bees wearing shakos. For those unfamiliar, the Spanish word *chaco* translates to the similar sounding *shako* in English. A shako is a military cap that is used during ceremonial guard by militaries and military academies in a variety of countries.

When the student needs to remember the list of monuments in order, he must first recall his list of peg words. The retrieval of the list of peg words will be aided by the rhyming relationship between each peg word and a number. Thus, for item number one, the student will retrieve *bun*, which is now associated with a bun-eating devil in a tower. This image will cue the first national monument established: Devils Tower. Item number two will be represented in memory by *shoe*—in this case, a shoe made of petrified wood. The image of a petrified shoe will cue the second national monument: the Petrified Forest. The third to-be-remembered item will be represented by *tree*, which is now associated with a castle-like tree house adorned with a large "M." This image will cue Montezuma Castle, which is the third national monument established. Item number four is represented by *door*, specifically a door made of carved rock and sandstone. This image will cue Inscription Rock. Finally, item number five is represented by *hive*. *Hive* will be associated with a hive in a canyon that is swarming with shako-wearing bees. This image will cue the fifth national monument established: Chaco Canyon.

Underlying Processes. Like the method of loci, the peg-word method involves a good deal of elaboration and organization, which should ultimately result in distinctive processing. All to-be-remembered items are organized serially by virtue of association with ordered numbers. Elaboration in the form of interactive mental imagery and association with the peg words should lead to high discriminability for the target information.

The image formed to assist in remembering Devils Tower is a fairly straightforward, though somewhat bizarre, interactive mental image. Developing this image requires relatively simple encoding because of the concrete nature of the monument's name. The image of shoes made of petrified wood used to remember the Petrified Forest is a highly interactive image that could be either common or bizarre depending on the type of shoe imaged. For example, whereas an image of wooden clogs would be relatively common, an image of wooden sneakers would be rather bizarre. The image of a castle atop a tree representing Montezuma Castle is another interactive image, but the association may require more rehearsal than the previous images because of the relatively weak cue for "Montezuma" (the "M" on the castle). Inscription Rock was represented by a door made of rocks and sandstone that had been carved upon. Like the image used for Montezuma Castle, the interactive image for Inscription Rock may require additional rehearsal if the learner has trouble with carvings as a cue for "Inscription." That is, the characteristics of the monument may be cued by this image, but the specific name may be more difficult to recover without additional rehearsal. The fifth national monument was represented by a bizarre interactive image of a hive in a canyon that was swarming with shako-wearing bees.

Examination of the processes underlying the use of the peg-word method reveals that the functional components are identical to those associated with the method of loci. Specifically, both induce distinctive processing by a combination of elaborative encoding and serial organization. In the present example, elaboration is the result of the association between each to-be-remembered item and a previously learned peg word, which is consolidated by the use of interactive mental imagery. Organization is exerted on the to-be-remembered information by virtue of the rhyming relationship between the peg words and a list of serial numbers. Ultimately, strong retrieval cues will be formed that should lead to mnemonic success.

Research Support. The peg-word method has been found to improve serial recall with both immediate and delayed testing (Elliott & Gentile, 1986; Wang & Thomas, 2000). Furthermore, research indicates that the method is effective for both normal and learning-disabled learners across a wide range of ages (Bugelski, 1968; Bugelski, Kidd, & Segmen, 1968; Elliott & Gentile, 1986; Krinsky & Krinsky, 1996; Veit, Scruggs, & Mastropieri, 1986; Wood & Pratt, 1987). Importantly, research (Massen & Vaterrodt-Plunnecke, 2006; Morris & Reid, 1970) also indicates that repeated use of a single list of peg words does not result in interference effects. However, category-relatedness among to-be-remembered items (Reddy & Bellezza, 1986) and rapid stimulus presentation (Bugelski et al., 1968) may reduce the effectiveness of the method.

☐ The Keyword Method

The keyword method was designed by Raugh and Atkinson (1975) specifically to enhance second-language acquisition. Unlike the method of loci and the peg-word method, the keyword method was designed not to enhance serial recall but to enhance cued recall. Specifically, the method was designed to aid memory for definitions when presented with foreign vocabulary. However, the application of the keyword method is not limited to second-language learning, as it can be useful for any vocabulary-learning situation.

Basic Procedures. The use of the keyword method begins with the definition and correct pronunciation of the vocabulary term to be learned. Next, the learner selects a word from her primary language that sounds similar to the correctly pronounced foreign word. This similar-sounding word will be considered the keyword. Finally, an interactive visual mental image between the keyword and the definition of the foreign word is created. When the foreign word to be defined is presented at testing, the pronunciation of the word will cue the previously formed interactive mental image, which contains a representation of the definition to be recalled.

Raugh and Atkinson (1975; see also Atkinson & Raugh, 1975) suggested that three criteria must be met in the selection of keywords. First, the keyword must sound as similar as possible to the foreign word. Although fulfilling this requirement can sometimes be difficult, Raugh and Atkinson noted that the keyword need not sound like the entire foreign word; similarity to part of the foreign word will suffice. For example, if the foreign word is polysyllabic, the keyword needs to sound similar to only one of the syllables. Also, the keyword does not necessarily have to be a single word at all—it can be an entire phrase. The second criterion in the selection of a keyword is that it lends itself to an easily formed interactive image with the definition of the foreign word. As such, concrete words or abstract words that can be easily represented by symbolic imagery will make the best keywords. The final criterion specified by Raugh and Atkinson is that a given keyword should be used for only one vocabulary term within a given list to be learned on a particular day. That is, although a given keyword should not be used more than once in a given learning session, a keyword used previously can be used again when learning a different list of vocabulary terms on a different day.

Example of Use. Suppose a Spanish student is having trouble learning the vocabulary terms *bigote, reina, arbol, lago,* and *tenedor.* The respective English translations of these words are *mustache, queen, tree, lake,* and *fork.* To remember that *bigote* means *moustache* using the keyword method, the student would first select an English word that sounds similar to the correct pronunciation of *bigote* (bee-goat-ay). In this case, it might be easiest to choose a keyword that sounds similar to one syllable of the Spanish word. For example, the student might choose the English word *goat* to use as the keyword. The student would then form an interactive image between the keyword and the definition of *bigote* such as a goat with a long handlebar moustache. The Spanish word *reina* is pronounced "rain-uh." Thus, to remember that *reina* means *queen,* the student could form a mental image of a queen standing in the rain. *Arbol* means *tree* and is pronounced "are-bowl." To remember this definition, the student could form a mental image of a tree growing out of a giant bowl. To remember that *lago* (pronounced "log-oh") means *lake,* the student could form an image of a log floating in a lake. *Tenedor* is pronounced "tay-nay-door." An image of a door impaled by a fork could be used to remember that *tenedor* means *fork.*

Memory for the definitions of the Spanish vocabulary terms will be cued by the pronunciation of each term. Thus, correct pronunciation of *bigote* will cue the keyword *goat* and the corresponding image of a goat with a moustache. By design, the image will contain the definition of the target Spanish word. Similarly, correct pronunciation of the other vocabulary terms will cue their respective keywords, which will be associated via mental imagery with their proper definitions.

Underlying Processes. The main underlying features of the keyword method are the elaborative and organizational properties of interactive mental imagery in addition to the phonemic–semantic relationships formed through selective encoding. As such, distinctive processing provides the foundation for this method.

All images formed when using the keyword method capitalize on a phonemic relationship between the keyword and the correct pronunciation of the target word as well as an association between the keyword and an English translation. However, there may be some slight variability in mnemonic properties of the images formed. For example, the images formed for remembering the meanings of *bigote* and *tenedor* were based on their most easily imaged syllables. Notice that for *tenedor* one could have used the keyword *neigh*, which corresponds to the second syllable of the term. However, *neigh* requires a secondary image (a horse) whereas the keyword *door* can be imaged directly. Also, the images used for *bigote, arbol*, and *tenedor* were relatively bizarre, whereas the images used for *lago* and *reina* were common. As has been noted previously, this mixture of common and bizarre imagery may enhance the effectiveness of the method.

Research Support. Empirical research has demonstrated the keyword method to be an effective strategy for learning vocabularies in languages such as Spanish (Raugh & Atkinson, 1975), Russian (Atkinson & Raugh, 1975), German (Desrochers, Wieland, & Cote, 1991), Chinese (Wang & Thomas, 1992), and Tagalog (Wang, Thomas, & Ouellette, 1992). The keyword method has also been shown to enhance vocabulary learning in one's primary language among both normal (Levin, Levin, Glasman, & Nordwall, 1992; Sweeney & Bellezza, 1982; Troutt-Ervin, 1990) and learning-disabled (Cundus, Marshall, & Miller, 1986; Mastropieri, Scruggs, & Fulk, 1990) populations.

In addition to enhancing vocabulary learning, the keyword method has been found to be effective in improving memory for other types of information such as that used by artists (Carney & Levin, 1991), in botany (Rosenheck, Levin, & Levin, 1989), and in music history (Brigham & Brigham, 1998).

Although the keyword method is generally considered an effective mnemonic, research has uncovered some potential limitations of the method. First, several studies (Thomas & Wang, 1996; Wang & Thomas, 1995; Wang, Thomas, Inzana, & Primicerio, 1993; Wang et al., 1992) suggest that the keyword method does not improve memory after a long retention interval (see Carney & Levin, 1998a, 2000a, for possible exceptions). Recent research (Worthen, Fontenelle, Deschamps, & Foreman, 2008) also suggests that the method is more effective with auditory than visual presentation of the to-be-learned information. Other research suggests that both verbal ability (Dretzke, 1993) and the quality of mental imagery (Beaton, Gruneburg, Hyde, Shufflebottom, & Sykes, 2005; Campos, Amor, & Gonzalez, 2004) may moderate the effectiveness of the method. Finally, research (van Hell & Mahn, 1997) indicates that rote memorization may be more effective than the keyword method for experienced foreign-language learners.

□ The Phonetic System

The phonetic system is a rather complicated system designed specifically to aid recall of numbers. It should be noted that this system is sometimes referred to as the digit–consonant method or the major system.

Basic Procedures. Based on the notion that words are easier to remember than numbers, the phonetic system involves converting numbers to letters, which are then combined to form words. The letters represent consonant sounds, and thus numbers zero through 9 are represented by one or more consonants. Vowels do not represent numbers but are used arbitrarily by the learner to create words for combinations of consonants. When the target number must be remembered, the word representing the number is recovered and then decoded back into numbers. Table 4.1 shows a typical representational scheme for the phonetic system.

TABLE 4.1 Typical Conversion of Letters to Numbers Using the Phonetic System

Number	Letter/Consonant Sound Representations
0	soft *c, s, z*
1	*d, t, th*
2	*n*
3	*m*
4	*r*
5	*l*
6	*ch,* soft *g, j*
7	hard *c,* hard *g, k, qu*
8	*f, ph, v*
9	*b, p*

Note: Vowels are used arbitrarily to form words.

Example of Use. Consider a situation in which a person wishes to purchase binoculars in order to pursue bird-watching (also known as "birding") as a new hobby. For novices, selecting binoculars can be a cumbersome task partially because the characteristics of binoculars are denoted by numbers. Typically, binoculars are specified in terms of power of magnification and the diameter of the objective lens (the lens farthest from the eye). As an example of a typical specification, the primary field binocular for the U.S. Marine Corps (the M25) is specified at 7×50. The first number represents the magnification, and the second number represents the diameter of the objective lens. Thus, the M25 has a magnification that results in an object appearing seven times closer than it is, and the objective lens is 50mm wide. The diameter of the objective lens is important because it determines the amount of ambient light gathered, which in turn determines the clarity of an image. As the diameter of the objective lens increases, more light can be gathered and images become clearer. However, binoculars with a large objective-lens diameter are generally larger and heavier than those with a small diameter.

Another number that must be considered when selecting binoculars is that associated with eye relief. Eye relief determines the distance one's eyes can be from the eyepiece without compromising the integrity of the image. A typical eye relief is 11mm; however, for those who wear eyeglasses, a relief of at least 14mm is usually necessary.

Let us say that the birder, after considering the intended uses of the binoculars, concludes that she needs binoculars that are easy to carry and have mid-range power. In addition, because she wears thick eyeglasses, she needs a good deal of eye relief. Ultimately, the birder decides to purchase 8×30 binoculars with a 15mm eye relief. Using the system described in Table 4.1, she can remember the specifications of the binoculars by converting 8×30 to the word *famous* and the number 15 to *tool*. Thus, the specifications of the binoculars can be represented by *famous tool*. In this case, 8 is represented by *f*, and 30 is represented by *ms*. The vowels *a*, *o*, and *u* are added to form the word *famous*. Similarly, the number 15 is represented by *t* and *l* with *os* added to form the word *tool*. When it comes time to remember the specifications of her binoculars, she need remember only her *famous tool* and then convert the letters back to numbers.

Underlying Processes. There are two main processes underlying the use of the phonetic system. First, transformational encoding is involved in the conversion of numbers to letters. Next these letters are elaborated on to construct words. Construction of concrete words that induce mental imagery should increase the distinctiveness of the new representation (Hunt & Marschark, 1987). However, the associative link between the to-be-remembered number and its word representation depends on correct reconversion to numbers. Although reconversion to numbers is also involved when using the peg-word method, in that case the rhyming relationship between each peg word and a serial number serves to aid reconversion. Moreover, this rhyming relationship decreases demands on memory for the list of peg words, which allows more cognitive resources to be available for the recovery of the target item. Unfortunately, the phonetic system does not have a built-in mechanism to reduce the cognitive load associated with either conversion or reconversion to numbers. For that reason, the cumbersome procedures of the system have the potential to outweigh the benefits of elaboration and mental imagery. Although some researchers (e.g., Bellezza, Six, & Phillips, 1992; Bower, 1978; Carney & Levin, 1994) have offered mnemonics to enhance memory for the phonetic conversions, it is unlikely that these procedures significantly reduce the difficulty of mastering the system.

Research Support. The results of initial research investigating the efficacy of the phonetic system were mixed. Bruce and Clemons (1982) found the method to be ineffective in enhancing memory for metric conversions and standard measurements. Similarly, Patton (1986) found that the phonetic system did not facilitate and sometimes hindered recall of dates, addresses, and phone numbers. Contrary to these results, Morris and Greer (1983) found the system to be effective for remembering lists of two-digit numbers. Subsequent research (Patton, D'Agaro, & Gaudette, 1991; Patton & Lanzy, 1987) provided clues to understanding the discrepancy in previous results by demonstrating that the effectiveness of the phonetic system depends on whether participants were supplied with conversions or generated conversions themselves. Specifically, these studies indicated that the system is effective when conversions are provided but not when they are self-generated. These findings are not surprising given the overall difficulty of use of the method.

Bellezza et al. (1992) pointed out that the original formulation of the phonetic system does not accommodate large numbers especially well. As a remedy to this problem, they suggested that long numbers be broken down into digit pairs that are each represented by a single word. A story is then constructed to link the words together in serial order. Although the authors demonstrated that these procedures led to strong memory for long strings of digits, it should be noted that the memory performance was best when components of the method of loci were also included in the procedures.

Research (e.g., Thompson, Cowan, & Frieman, 1993; Wilding & Valentine, 1994) has suggested that the phonetic system is frequently used by those with exceptional memory skills. One could interpret this to mean that the phonetic system can lead to exceptional memory performance. On the other hand, given the overall complexity and difficulty of use of this method, this finding could be interpreted to suggest that exceptional cognitive ability is necessary for effective use of the method. Supporting the former argument, Higbee (1997) demonstrated that with a good deal of training, even novices can demonstrate feats of memory similar to those of mnemonists. Regardless, in keeping with the conclusions of Patton and Lanzy (1987), the phonetic system is likely to be impractical and possibly ineffective for casual purposes.

Summary and Conclusions

Examination of our sample of popular formal mnemonics indicates that the effectiveness of even complex mnemonics results from a combination of a few basic cognitive processes. Distinctive processing resulting from the interplay of elaboration and organization is particularly fundamental to mnemonic success. Mental imagery also plays an important role, due to having both elaborative and organizational properties. Knowledge of the processes underlying mnemonic effectiveness is important to both those who are interested in using formal mnemonics and those who wish to devise their own. In the former case, knowledge of the processes will allow one to tweak mnemonics devised by others without inadvertently diminishing effectiveness. For those interested in new mnemonic techniques, knowledge of the underlying processes provides the tools necessary for creating effective learning procedures.

Organizational Mnemonics

The main purpose of organizational mnemonics is to organize to-be-remembered information in a way that facilitates remembering. Although we noted the importance of organization in preceding chapters, we have also argued that the mnemonic benefits of organization are fully realized only when it is combined with elaboration in a way that results in distinctive processing. Thus, mnemonics that rely predominantly on organization may be helpful in some situations, but their effectiveness is often limited unless they also incorporate mechanisms that encourage elaboration. In this chapter, we discuss mnemonics that rely solely on organization as well as mnemonics that serve primarily to organize information but also encourage a degree of elaboration.

☐ Acronym Mnemonics

Simple Acronyms. Creating an acronym out of the first letter of each to-be-remembered item of a list is a rather popular organizational technique. Frequently used by college students (Stalder, 2005), acronym mnemonics serve to reduce a list of to-be-remembered items into a single unit by representing each item in terms of its initial letter. For example, consider a nursing student who wishes to memorize the five stages of grief as suggested by Elisabeth Kubler-Ross (1969). According to Kubler-Ross, the first stage of the grief process is denial. During the denial stage, a person deals with distressing news by refusing to accept its veracity. After initial denial, the person may react with anger. It is during the anger stage that a person often wonders why the event causing the grief has occurred and then attempts to assign blame. In the bargaining stage, a person might appeal to a higher power for a reprieve from the unpleasant situation. The depressive stage typically follows the bargaining stage. During this stage, the person may feel hopeless as the result of overgeneralization of a real or perceived lack of control of the grief-inducing event. The final stage of the grief process is acceptance. It is during this stage when a person may address the situation philosophically and attempt to make the best of the situation.

Using an acronym mnemonic, learners can reduce the five stages of grief into a single phonemic unit: "DABDA." This acronym could potentially aid memory in two ways. First, the five stages are reduced into a single chunk, which should reduce cognitive load during retrieval. Second, this particular method of chunking should increase the probability of accurate serial recall because the phases of grief are serially organized within the context of the phonemic association.

Despite these potential advantages, a simple acronym mnemonic has deficiencies that limit its effectiveness. First, like the example above, most to-be-remembered lists result in an acronym that represents a phonemic unit that is void of meaning. That is, the acronym reduces the list by chunking, but the result is typically a nonsense word. Although this problem can be occasionally remedied by rearranging the order of the initial letters, this solution can complicate serial recall. With the acronyms resulting from this method being essentially meaningless, the possibilities of semantic elaboration and the use of mental imagery are greatly reduced. Although the method does lead to some nonmeaningful elaboration, it is clear that a simple acronym mnemonic does not strongly encourage distinctive processing. In line with these arguments, empirical research suggests that the use of simple acronym mnemonics is of limited effectiveness (e.g., Carlson, Zimmer, & Glover, 1981; Kovar & Van Pelt, 1991) if not completely ineffective (e.g., Boltwood & Blick, 1970; Gruneberg, 1973; Waite, Blick, & Boltwood, 1971).

Embellished Acronyms. Stalder (2005) attempted to enhance the effectiveness of the simple acronym mnemonic by adding extraneous letters to acronyms in an effort to make them more meaningful. As an example, consider a situation in which one must learn the periods of Piaget's (1928) theory of cognitive development. According to this theory, cognitive development proceeds serially through four relatively discrete periods. During the first period, the sensorimotor period, a child's thinking is mainly focused on and initiated by external stimuli and action events. As a child enters the preoperational period, thinking becomes more independent of action, but it is marked by logical errors. During the concrete operations period, a child's thinking becomes increasingly logical, but the logical thinking does not extend to tasks that require abstract reasoning. Finally, during the formal operations period, the ability to handle abstract problems through logical thinking is achieved. To facilitate memory for these stages of cognitive development, Stalder suggested the use of the acronym "SPaCeFarm" whereby the four developmental periods are represented by the letters *S*, *P*, *C*, and *F*. Note that without additional let-ters, no meaningful acronym can be made by the initial letters of the peri-ods of development. However, the inclusion of extraneous letters allows the acronym to become meaningful, amenable to further elaboration, and easily imagined. Thus, by complementing the inherent organizational properties of the simple acronym mnemonic with meaningful elaboration and mental imagery, the embellished acronym mnemonic should encour-age distinctive processing and thus be more successful than a simple acronym. Stalder's results support these arguments by showing that those who used embellished acronyms demonstrated better exam performance than those who did not. However, the enhanced performance occurred only for material for which acronyms were provided and did not extend to nonacronym-related test items.

Another type of embellished acronym mnemonic involves creating a word from the initial letter of each to-be-remembered word and con-structing a phrase or story around those words. For example, an embel-lished acronym can be used to remember the 12 cranial nerves. The 12 cranial nerves are the optic, olfactory, oculomotor, trochlear, trigeminal, abducens, facial, auditory, glossopharyngeal, vagus, spinal accessory, and hypoglossal nerves. To remember these nerves one could use the embel-lished acronym: "On Old Olympus Towering Tops, A Finn And German Viewed Some Hops." This mnemonic adds a good deal of elaboration to the inherent organizational properties of the acronym and is amenable to mental imagery. As a result, it is likely to encourage distinctive processing and thus effectively enhance memory. Unfortunately, there are no pub-lished empirical studies that specifically evaluate this type of embellished mnemonic as differentiated from other acronym mnemonics. Clearly, there is need for research in this area. Additional examples of simple and embellished acronyms can be found in Table 5.1.

Other Considerations. Although there are some advantages to using acro-nym mnemonics (especially embellished acronyms), it should be noted that organizational mnemonics of this class serve mainly to enhance the intraitem associations among to-be-remembered items. Thus, the retrieval of a single item should cue retrieval of all succeeding items. On the other hand, the dependence on intraitem associations opens the possibility that failure to retrieve a single to-be-remembered item may negatively affect retrieval of all succeeding items. As such, recall of information using acro-nym mnemonics tends to be more "all or nothing" than other mnemonics.

It should also be noted that there is sometimes quite a leap between the cue provided by the acronym and a to-be-remembered item. For example, although the embellishment involved in the acronym for remembering the cranial nerves may result in a memorable phrase, the phrase does not provide strong cues for to-be-remembered items. That is, "German" does not result in an obvious association with "glossopharyngeal." Thus,

---

TABLE 5.1 Examples of Acronyms

Simple (Not Meaningful)

BEDMAS: Brackets, Exponents, Division, Multiplication, Addition, Subtraction—the order of mathematical operations.

IPMAT: Interphase, Prophase, Metaphase, Anaphase, Telophase—the stages of cell division.

SIGECAPS: Sleep disturbance, Interest (diminished), Guilt, Energy loss, Concentration difficulties, Appetite abnormalities, Psychomotor retardation or agitation, Suicidal ideation—the symptoms of major depression.

Simple (Meaningful)

BRASS: Breathe, Relax, Aim, Sight, Squeeze trigger—process of shooting a rifle.

D-CUP: Describe, Control, Understand, and Predict—the goals of science. Note that these goals are not in proper order.

HOMES: Huron, Ontario, Michigan, Eerie, and Superior—the Great Lakes.

Embellished (With Letters)

ARrOW: Airworthiness certificate, Registration certificate, Operating handbook, Weight and balance information—paperwork required to be on board during a flight.

CATARAct: Congenital, Aging, Toxicity, Accidents, Radiation, Abnormal metabolism—the causes of cataracts.

GrAPHS: Glider, Angular, Pivotal, Hinge, Suture—types of human joints.

---

it may be that some sort of interactive imagery between each cue and target is needed for maximal effectiveness of acronym mnemonics. With the addition of such interactive imagery, embellished acronyms would be functionally similar to the peg-word method whereby the acronym would serve as a framework that provides both cue-to-cue and cue-to-target associations.

☐ Story Mnemonics

Constructing a story around to-be-remembered information is another mnemonic technique that emphasizes intraitem associations. However, the story mnemonic has an advantage over an embellished acronym mnemonic because in the former mnemonic the actual target items are used in the construction of a story whereas in the latter a proxy is used in the construction of a story. As such, the story mnemonic eliminates the step of having to remember which to-be-remembered item is associated with each component of the story. However, not all lists are amenable to the story mnemonic. For example, the story mnemonic would be of little help in remembering the cranial nerves without using an acronym and mediators. Nonetheless, the story mnemonic has potential to be very effective for learning relatively common information in serial order.

As an example of use of the story mnemonic, consider a situation in which a person must remember a to-do list in preparation for a lengthy trip away from home. Specifically, our traveler must remember to take her dog to the kennel, stop newspaper delivery to her home, withdraw cash from the bank, pick up dresses from the dry cleaner, and pay bills prior to departure. An effective use of the story mnemonic in this situation would first involve identification of a cue for each task on the list. Proper cue selection is important when using the story mnemonic because the cues chosen must not only bring to mind the appropriate to-be-remembered items but also combine in a way that allows for meaningful story construction. For our example, let us use *dog* to cue "take the dog to kennel," *newspaper* to cue "stop newspaper delivery," *bank* to cue "withdraw cash from the bank," *dry cleaning* to cue "pick up dresses from the dry cleaner," and *bills* to cue "pay bills." To remember these tasks, the traveler can construct a short story including these cues: "While walking the *dog*, I bought a *newspaper* and read that a *bank* had been robbed. Apparently, the robbers needed the money to pay their *dry cleaning bills*." This story provides a meaningful consolidation of all cues in such a way that maintains the serial order of the list. In addition, each cue is strongly associated with its respective to-be-remembered task. Thus, we have achieved both strong cue-to-cue and strong cue-to target associations. Moreover, these cues are embellished within a meaningful context that lends itself to visual mental imagery. As such, this example demonstrates how the story mnemonic can easily incorporate organization and elaboration to induce distinctive processing, which should effectively facilitate remembering.

Empirical research supports the notion that constructing a story out of to-be-remembered items can be a highly effective mnemonic. The story mnemonic has been demonstrated to be effective in facilitating memory in both college-age (e.g., Herrmann, 1987; Herrmann, Geisler, & Atkinson, 1973) and older (e.g., Drevenstedt & Bellezza, 1993; Hill, Allen, & McWhorter, 1991) adults. In addition, the story mnemonic has been shown to be effective in improving memory in memory-impaired (Wilson, 1995) and mildly retarded (Glidden, 1983) participants. It should also be noted that story mnemonics can be effective both with long lists (Bellezza, Six, & Phillips, 1992) and over long retention intervals (Drevenstedt & Bellezza, 1993). Moreover, the effectiveness of the story mnemonic does not differ when self-generated and other-generated stories are compared (Buonassissi, Blick, & Kibler, 1972). However, as we alluded to earlier, the effectiveness of the story mnemonic may be reduced when the to-be-remembered information is particularly abstract (Manning & Bruning, 1975).

☐ Mnemonics of Rhyme and Rhythm

Simple Rhymes. The construction of simple rhymes to enhance recall is a common, though infrequently researched, mnemonic technique. The rationale behind the use of such a mnemonic is that a rhyme scheme allows to-be-remembered information to be organized based on phonemic similarities. However, because to-be-remembered items do not always share rhyming relationships, mnemonic rhymes are often used to provide a context in which target items are embedded. For example, consider an age-old mnemonic designed to help people remember how to distinguish the North American coral snake from the scarlet king snake. The North American coral snake is a highly venomous snake that can be identified by red-, yellow-, and black-colored banding. The harmless and often beneficial king snake also has red, yellow, and black bands, but the bands appear in a different order than those of the coral snake. Specifically, the North American coral snake always has yellow bands that separate the black and red bands. On the other hand, the yellow bands on the scarlet king snake always occur between black bands. As such, the following mnemonic can be used to help distinguish the snakes: "Red on yellow, kill a fellow; red on black, friend of Jack."

A similar, but more folkloric, rhyme mnemonic has been used to help sailors make weather predictions: "Red sky at night, sailor's delight. Red sky in morning, sailor's warning." The bases for this mnemonic are that weather systems usually move from west to east and that red skies result in part from the illumination of moisture-bearing clouds. If red clouds are seen in the evening, then the clear western sky is allowing the sun to illuminate moisture-bearing clouds moving out of the area toward the east. However, if red clouds are seen in the morning, then the clear eastern sky is allowing the sun to illuminate moisture-bearing clouds that will be arriving from the west. Thus, a red sky at night means weather systems are departing, and red skies in the morning means that a system will be arriving.

Simple rhyme mnemonics such as these are designed to help one avoid confusion in situations where incorrect memories could have damaging consequences. One can easily imagine a situation in which a person remembers that the appearance of coral snakes and king snakes differs based on red, yellow, and black banding yet fails to remember which banding is associated with which snake. Similarly, one might recall that a red sky in the morning signifies something about the weather while being unable to remember what the red sky portends. Embedding important information in the context of a rhyme provides an organization that greatly constrains the number of correct retrieval possibilities. As such, this type of rhyme mnemonic should significantly reduce memory errors. Moreover, because rhyme mnemonics typically require elaboration to associate the target information to phonemically related information, distinctive processing can be induced. On the other hand, rhyme mnemonics encourage selective encoding that minimizes semantics in favor of phonemic features. As mentioned in Chapter 3, this type of encoding would be less effective than encoding that encourages semantic elaboration.

Although very little research has directly examined the effectiveness of simple rhyme mnemonics, the existing research and that research that examines the relationship between rhyme and memory more generally suggest that rhyme mnemonics may be of limited effectiveness. Hayes, Chemelski, and Palmer (1982) found that rhymes enhanced memory for adults but not for young children. In a follow-up study testing young children only, Johnson and Hayes (1987) demonstrated that rhymes enhance verbatim recitation of stories but failed to facilitate recall of gist. The failure of rhymes to enhance memory for gist in young children is presumably due to perceptual centration that results from the selective encoding of phonemic cues. On the other hand, the recall advantage associated with rhymes found with adults is believed to be due to the restrictions rhymes impose on retrieval possibilities (e.g., Bower & Bolton, 1969; Wallace & Rubin, 1991). Other research testing adults (e.g., Rubin & Wallace, 1989; Solso & Biersdorff, 1975) indicates that rhyme cues are most effective when presented in combination with semantic cues. The same is true for mentally challenged adults (Javawardhana, 1997).

The combination of rhyme and meaning conforms to the prescription that effective mnemonics include both organization and elaboration. The rhyme provides the shared information to organize discrete elements, whereas the semantic information distinguishes among the various elements. Rubin and Wallace (1989; Wallace & Rubin, 1991) explained the effectiveness of the combined dimensions as cue constraint. In effect, the suggestion is that a combination is distinctive because few alternatives will satisfy that combination. For example, once learned, the nursery rhyme Jack and Jill is easily remembered because the rhyme-meaning constraint severely limits the critical word choices. It is a hill that Jack and Jill go up, and the constraints are such that neither stairs nor mountain will come to mind.

Rhyme and Rhythm. Rhyme and rhythm are often used in combination to form mnemonics. In his book *Memory in Oral Traditions: The Cognitive Psychology of Epic, Ballads, and Counting-Out Rhymes*, Rubin (1995) provided in-depth coverage of the functions of rhyme and rhythms on memory. Rubin suggested the mechanism underlying the effectiveness of rhyme and rhythm is the same as that for rhyme and meaning. That is, when attempting to recall information that was learned in a rhyming and/or rhythmic context, any recalled information that does not fit with the rhyme scheme or does not maintain proper rhythm can be easily determined to be incorrect. Thus, rhyme and rhythm facilitate memory by limiting the potential retrieval set. The functions of rhyme and rhythm described by Rubin are not unlike the function of distinctive processing. Specifically, distinctive processing results from an organized context complemented by unique cues. Organization specifies the appropriate episodic context, and item-specific cues limit retrieval possibilities to items that both share the unique cue and match the specified context (Hunt & Smith, 1996). Although Rubin discussed the constraints imposed by rhyme and rhythm mainly in terms of retrieval, it must be kept in mind that retrieval is highly dependent on encoding. As such, a strong distinction between encoding and retrieval processes is generally untenable (cf. Tulving, 1983).

When rhyme and rhythm are combined with melody, to-be-remembered information becomes lyrics to a song. Under some conditions information presented in the context of a song is remembered better than when in the context of simple speech. For example, Wallace (1994) found that text presented in the context of a simple melody is remembered better than text alone as long as the melody is repeated. According to Wallace, repetition is important to the mnemonic benefits of song because it makes the melody easier to learn, which ultimately enhances its familiarity. It should also be noted that Wallace's results also indicated that the observed benefits of song exceeded the benefits of rhyme alone.

More recent research (Kilgour, Jakobson, & Cuddy, 2000) suggests that the mnemonic benefits of embedding to-be-remembered information in song found in previous research may be due to slower presentation rates associated with songs than speech. Indeed, when these authors equated the presentation rates of information presented in songs and speech, the advantage of song was eliminated. Regardless of this finding, it is clear that large amounts of information can be recalled accurately when embedded in song (see Wallace & Rubin, 1988).

☐ Categorical and Schematic Organization

A simple way to organize to-be-remembered information is to arrange the information in a taxonomic hierarchy. This type of mnemonic capitalizes on categorical relationships among list items by organizing the to-be-remembered list into subsets that can be subsumed under abstract category labels. Revisiting our earlier example of a person who is preparing for travel, let us say she must also remember to pack the following items: hair dryer, dental floss, hand lotion, MP3 player, magazine, puzzle book, business cards, laptop computer, and jump drive. To remember these items, our traveler could organize the nine items into three ad hoc categories: toiletries, entertainment items, and work-related items. Prior to departing for her trip, the traveler may attempt to recall the items and verify that they have been packed. Using the categorical mnemonic, the traveler simply needs to recall the three category labels, which should cue the specific items that are subsumed under each label. Note that this method reduces cognitive load by decreasing the overall number of items that must be retrieved without cues. The categorical mnemonic is also advantageous in this situation because recall of the category label may cue additional items that may be needed for the trip but did not appear on the original list. Thus, when applied to this situation, recall intrusions—which are common with a categorical mnemonic—are actually helpful.

As an alternative to a categorical mnemonic, the traveler could use schematic organization to help her remember items that she must pack. For example, she could mentally visit each room in her apartment and gather the necessary items found in each room. For example, the hair dryer, dental floss, and hand lotion may be cued by the mental image of the bathroom; the MP3 player, magazine, and puzzle book may be cued by the living room; and the business cards, laptop, and jump drive may be cued by the office nook. Note that the schematic mnemonic differs from the categorical mnemonic in that the former cues to-be-remembered items based on spatial relationships, whereas the latter cues items based on semantic–conceptual relationships. However, like the categorical mnemonic, semantic organization allows for additional, but previously unconsidered, items to be recalled. The recall intrusions associated with this method and the categorical mnemonic can be explained by a lack of item-specific processing that would be necessary to discriminate target items from other items that fit within the schema or category. A potential limitation of the schematic mnemonic is that items that are typically concealed from view (e.g., dental floss that is stored in a cabinet or a drawer) may be overlooked during the mental inventory (Keenan, 1983; Kerr & Neisser, 1983).

Empirical research (Khan & Paivio, 1988; Nakamura, Kleiber, & Kim, 1992) suggests that categorical organization and schematic organization lead to equivalent levels of recall and that each exceeds the level of recall in control conditions. However, it may be the case that children do not obtain the mnemonic benefits of categorical and schematic organization realized by adults. This notion is supported by research that suggests that lists organized by categories lead to better recall than randomly constructed lists in adults (Bower, Clark, Lesgold, & Winzenz, 1969) but not in young children (Yoshimura, Moely, & Shapiro, 1971). Moreover, research (Liberty & Ornstein, 1973) suggests that young children do not spontaneously organize to-be-remembered information. These findings are consistent with the notion that young children have a limited capacity for abstract thinking, which prevents them from forming meaningful categories and schemas (Piaget, 1928).

☐ Advance Organizers

An advance organizer is a typically other-generated mnemonic that strongly reflects a categorical and/or schematic organization. Unlike some mnemonics, advance organizers are specifically designed to facilitate memory for lengthy prose and technical discourse. For this reason, advance organizers are perfectly suited for educational applications.

Originally promoted by Ausubel (1960), advance organizers are concepts provided prior to relevant reading material in order to facilitate learning. Ausubel's advance organizers were concepts under which subsequent information could be subsumed. According to this formulation, the information provided in advance serves to activate knowledge in a way that enhances links between that knowledge and new information. Ausubel described two types of advance organizers that can be used: comparative and expository. Comparative organizers are used when the learner has some background knowledge relevant to the to-be-learned material. This type of organizer is used to aid memory for concepts that, although fundamentally different, share similarities with previously learned concepts. Thus, the main function of a comparative advance organizer is to allow the learner to discriminate between two similar concepts. For example, an anthropology instructor might provide students with a short passage describing the relationship between modern American and Native American burial rites prior to a reading assignment that details traditional burial practices of Native Americans. It is assumed here that the students would be familiar with modern American burial practices but not the Native American practices. As such, the advance organizer would serve to activate previous knowledge about burial practices in a way that establishes a basis for comparison and contrast with the new information.

Expository advance organizers are appropriate for situations in which the learner has little or no background relevant to the to-be-learned topic. Thus, the purpose of an expository advance organizer is to create a cognitive network that will allow for the subsequent categorization of the new information. For instance, a kinesiology instructor teaching an introductory archery course might present students with the four main components of proper shooting form (stance, draw, aim, and release) prior to an assigned reading on the details of shot accuracy. This advance organizer would provide the learner with a basic cognitive framework that would allow for the subsumption of detailed information under four main category labels. In essence, the organizer presents the "big picture" associated with bow-shooting accuracy prior to presenting the technical details. It should be noted that modern expository advance organizers are often designed simply to provide a minimum framework for the assimilation of new information (see Langan-Fox, Platania-Phung, & Waycott, 2006;

Mayer, 2003). As such, many modern advance organizers take the form of flowcharts, concept maps, or conceptual models.

A good deal of research has been conducted on the effectiveness of advance organizers on learning and memory. Although there is some variability in the conclusions of that research (see Corkill, 1992), the consensus is that the use of advance organizers can be beneficial for learning verbal material given that certain conditions are met. Of course, advance organizers must be well written and relevant to the to-be-learned topic area (Glover, Krug, Dietzer, & George, 1990). Moreover, organizers that represent concepts concretely will be more effective than those that represent concepts abstractly (Corkill, Bruning, & Glover, 1988). The learning environment in which organizers will be implemented must be free from distractions, as advance organizers do not compensate for impoverished learning conditions (Stallings & Derry, 1986). Research (Glover et al., 1990) has also demonstrated that although memory in three advance organizer conditions exceeded that of a control condition, organizers introduced an hour prior to target material were more effective than those introduced immediately prior or 48 hours prior to the memory test. The effectiveness of advance organizers is also enhanced by long retention intervals (Allen, 1970; Wong, 1974). In addition, Corkill, Glover, Bruning, and Krug (1988) found that the mnemonic benefits of advance organizers were enhanced by rereading the organizers prior to delayed testing. Addressing individual differences, research by Thompson (1998) suggests that advance organizers enhance memory for learners with low verbal abilities across a wide range of adult ages. However, it should be noted that this study found that advance organizers benefited recognition memory but not recall in normal older adults. Finally, regarding advance organizers, it should be noted that in keeping with distinctiveness theory, their effectiveness is significantly increased when used in combination with procedures that encourage elaboration (Van Dam, Brinkerink-Carlier, & Kok, 1985).

☐ Summary

All of the mnemonic techniques described in this chapter can be effective as long as their limitations are considered and they are applied to an appropriate situation. Acronyms are not particularly effective unless they are amenable to mental imagery and/or embellished with semantic elaboration. Story mnemonics involve a good deal of elaboration, and as a result, they are a very effective type of organizational mnemonic. Unfortunately, not all to-be-learned information lends itself to meaningful story construction. Like acronyms, rhyme mnemonics are most effective when combined with other forms of elaboration. When simple rhymes are combined with rhythm and melody, the result is an effective mnemonic. Categorical and schematic mnemonics are highly susceptible to recall intrusions, but this problem can be used to one's advantage when such mnemonics are applied to situations in which intrusions can be helpful. Under certain conditions, advance organizers induce processing that leads to effective categorical and schematic organization.

Overall, it is clear that the effectiveness of an organizational mnemonic depends on the degree elaboration involved. When organizational procedures are combined with elaboration, the mnemonic is generally effective. Without elaboration, distinctive processing is minimized, and the effectiveness of an organizational mnemonic will depend on whether the learning situation requires target-item discriminability. In situations where memory for gist is acceptable and recall intrusions are not problematic, mnemonics that rely predominantly on organization may be helpful. However, when the discriminability of to-be-remembered information is crucial, mnemonics that are predominantly organizational may be of limited effectiveness.

Experts and Professional Mnemonists

Like most other abilities, memory skill lies on a continuum that approximates a normal distribution. A small proportion of the population will suffer from marked memory deficits, most people's memory will fall within a range that we consider normal, and another small proportion will exhibit particularly strong memory skills. The present chapter focuses on this latter end of the continuum of memory ability. Specifically, we will discuss four individuals whose feats of memory represent deviation from the norm that can be considered truly exceptional. The individuals discussed in this chapter by no means exhaust the list of those who have exhibited exceptional memory ability. However, the sample does reflect the variability in backgrounds, methods, and abilities that exists among those who have superior general memory.

☐ S.

Although empirical examination of individuals with exceptional memory skills dates back to the 19th century (Brown & Deffenbacher, 1975; Wilding & Valentine, 1997), Luria's (1968) study of S. was the first to garner widespread attention. S. was a curious case partly because he had no awareness of his special abilities until his late 20s when an employer suggested that psychological researchers should study his memory ability. Furthermore, other than his unusual cognitive abilities, S. was, for the most part, functionally average or slightly below average. His family life was typical—he was married and had a son who was later successful, yet he drifted from job to job without ever establishing a stable career (except for that as a mnemonist). In this regard, Luria described S. as "anchorless" in that he lived his life always in anticipation of a future event that would alter the course of his existence.

S. demonstrated exceptional ability for the typically difficult task of remembering arrays of random numbers and letters. As an example, Luria (1968) stated that S., after less than 3 minutes study time, could accurately recall an array of 50 numbers in the order they were presented, backward, by rows, by columns, or even by specified diagonals. Another particularly striking example comes from what S. believed was his most difficult memory task. During performances as a mnemonist, S. would ask the audience to provide a list of to-be-remembered information that he would use to demonstrate his ability. On one particular occasion while performing at a sanitarium, S. was presented with a long series of alternating nonsense syllables such as that found in Table 6.1. Luria reported that not only did S. accurately recall the list at the performance but he also managed to reproduce, from memory, the entire list 4 years later.

In addition to his ability with numbers, letters, and nonsense syllables, S. also demonstrated exceptional memory for words. However, his memory for verbal material did not necessarily extend to meaningful prose. In fact, Luria (1968) suggested that S. had a particularly difficult time understanding the content of text. He also had difficulty remembering faces. These difficulties were at least partly due to an extreme form of synesthesia that S. sometimes found to be debilitating. For instance, S. reported that simple sounds induced vivid mental imagery, color, and taste. Numbers and visual forms had similar multimodal effects. As a result, even simple information stimulated all of his senses, which made extracting meaning very difficult for him. It was as if meaning was just a detail embedded in the vast perceptual experience associated with any

---

TABLE 6.1 Partial List of Nonsense Syllables Presented to S. at a Performance in 1936

ma va na sa na va

na sa na ma va

sa na ma na va

va sa na va na ma

na va na va sa ma

na ma sa ma va na

sa ma sa va na

na sa ma va ma na

Note: Actual list was longer than what appears in the table. Adapted from Luria, A. R., 1968, *The Mind of a Mnemonist*, Basic Books, New York.

---

given stimulus. Moreover, Luria stated that S. had great difficulty with words whose meanings did not seem to match their synesthetic qualities. If a word did not match what the sound of the word suggested, S. became confused. Clearly, S.'s cognitive functioning was not normal, and this deviation from normality was not always adaptive.

Common to discussions of extraordinary memory ability is the issue of whether the ability is innate or the result of practice (see Chase & Ericsson, 1982; Ericsson, 1985; Wilding & Valentine, 1991). Arguments for the latter stem from research (Ericsson, Chase, & Falloon, 1980) in which a purportedly average man (SF) increased his digit span to 82 digits through practice. However, Wilding and Valentine (1997) argued that even if SF was normal in IQ and memory prior to the study, he most certainly had exceptional drive and motivation. In fact, Wilding and Valentine describe the SF's desire to succeed in several areas of his life as "almost obsessional" (p. 35). Regardless, we believe that the debate over innate versus practiced ability is not particularly relevant. As discussed in earlier chapters, the effectiveness of mnemonics is moderated by individual differences, and thus truly exceptional memory ability is not within the grasp of all who are willing to learn even the most effective mnemonic techniques. Of course, we believe that mnemonics can be helpful and result in significant memory improvement. However, potential effectiveness of a given mnemonic technique is constrained by the nature of the learning task and both the innate and environmentally derived characteristics of the learner. Thus, in our view, the relevant issue is not whether superior memory is innate or learned but whether the strategies employed by those with exceptional memory ability can be helpful to the average learner. With this in mind, we will now discuss the mnemonic techniques used by S.

Although Luria (1968) concluded that S.'s ability was innate, it is clear that S. used some mnemonic techniques. Visual mental imagery was an interminable and perhaps uncontrollable component of S.'s encoding. Also, because of his synesthesia, the use of multiple codes and abundant elaboration were also constants to his encoding process. S. also made extensive use of the method of loci. When presented with a long list of words, S. would imagine walking down a familiar street in Moscow and then place mental images of the to-be-remembered items in various places. When he needed to recall the information, he would again imagine walking down the street, this time gathering the items he left behind. As noted by Luria, this explains why S. had no trouble recalling information in reverse order. When asked to recall a list backward, he would simply begin his mental walk down the opposite end of the street.

Interestingly, S. was not immune to the difficulties that sometimes arise when using the method of loci. For example, he might have trouble remembering a to-be-remembered item if he had mentally placed it in a poorly lit or concealed place. This is keeping with researchers (Iaccino &

Byrne, 1989; Keenan & Moore, 1979) who have argued that concealed mental imagery leads to poorer recall than unconcealed imagery. In Chapter 4, we discussed research that generally supports the notion that the ability to recall concealed images depends on the time available to form images. In support of this, Luria suggested that S.'s performance was optimal when lists were not presented rapidly. It is also interesting to note that S. reported that he frequently transformed the image size of small to-be-remembered items so that they did not get "lost" in the detailed landscape of his imagined place. Image-size transformation is one of several operations that have been used to create bizarre imagery (Marshall, Nau, & Chandler, 1979) that, as we discussed earlier, may be used to enhance the effectiveness of some mnemonics.

Notwithstanding his difficulties with concealed images, S. clearly made more effective use of the method of loci than would the average person. This raises an interesting question about the use of the mnemonic: Did S. use the method of loci differently than most users? For the most part, he did not. The same factors that underlie the effectiveness of the method for a typical user were functional when S. implemented the method. The main difference between S.'s use and that of any other person was his uncanny ability to create vivid and detailed mental images. In addition, it is likely that his synesthesia combined with the method of loci in such a way that resulted in particularly strong and effective distinctive processing. Synesthesia undoubtedly produces a uniquely effective form of item-specific processing that would be perfectly complemented by the organizational properties of a detailed mental image of a familiar place. As a result, it is likely that S.'s psychological makeup was simply more conducive for the effective use of the method of loci than is that of an average person.

S. also used a technique similar to the keyword method to remember words from a foreign language or phrases he could not comprehend. As described by Luria (1968), S. would create an image based on the pronunciation or even the synesthetic acoustics of a foreign word or phrase and then combine that image with something meaningful to enhance recall. When presented with long lists or phrases, S. would construct a story to create a chain of associations that would link the to-be-remembered items together. Again, S.'s unusually strong synesthesia-induced elaboration was a perfect complement to the organizational properties of the story method. Thus, it is no surprise that S. used this hybrid mnemonic with extreme effectiveness.

The exceptional memory ability of S. appears to have been at least partly the result of strong distinctive processing. This distinctive processing arose from a combination of profuse and seemingly automatic elaboration and common mnemonic techniques. In keeping with Luria's (1968) suggestion, it is almost certain that S. was born with uncommon cognitive processing. This unusual cognition resulted in amazing feats of memory but was at other times maladaptive. Regardless, one must concede that, in the very least, S. refined his already exceptional memory ability by using simple mnemonic techniques that could be used by an average person.

☐ V. P.

On the basis of the results of a variety of tests of memory ability (Hunt & Love, 1972), V. P. demonstrated memory ability that rivaled that of S. However, V. P.'s memory was more versatile than S.'s in that the former displayed exceptional memory for not only numbers and nonsense syllables but also phrases, stories, and chess positions. Moreover, V. P. had no trouble comprehending meaning. Apparently, V. P. demonstrated superior memory at an early age as exemplified by memorizing a map of the Latvian city of Riga at age 5 and memorizing 150 poems as part of a competition at age 10 (Wilding & Valentine, 1997). V. P. was generally considered more intelligent than S., as indicated by his proficiency with several languages and IQ of 136 (Wilding & Valentine, 1997).

   Unfortunately, there is not much information about the specific techniques V. P. used in his attempts to remember. Hunt and Love (1972) suggested that he did not possess extraordinary imagery or spatial skills; however, as mentioned by Wilding and Valentine (1997), this is not consistent with his memorization of the map of Riga. The only explanations given for his superior memory were the use of meaningful associations and, according to V. P. himself, extensive practice with rote memorization while in school. Given the lack of information (self-reported or otherwise) about V. P.'s methods of memorization, we will keep our discussion of him brief. However, we believed it important to include V. P. in this chapter because he is frequently used as a basis for comparison in discussions of other individuals with superior memory owing to the fact that his ability was examined more empirically than was S.'s.

☐ Aitken

At face value, the case of Alexander Aitken appears to be in stark contrast to that of Luria's (1968) S. As described by Hunter (1977), Aitken was an astute mental calculator and successful mathematician with an outstanding memory for numbers. As an example, he learned pi to 1,000 places and had a digit span of 13 to 15 items. Furthermore, Hunter described him as a consummate intellectual with a broad knowledge base and a keen interest in the underlying meaning of all things. Unlike S., Aitken exhibited strong memory for meaningful information including passages of prose and musical notation. Aitken claimed to have memorized the books of Virgil and Milton's *Paradise Lost* during his school days. Although these facts paint a picture that seems quite different from Luria's description of S., Hunter's concerted effort to emphasize the differences between S. and Aitken may have obscured some important similarities between the two. It is quite evident in Hunter's article that he believed that Aitken's abilities and accomplishments were qualitatively superior to S.'s. This sentiment permeates his discussion of Aitken and is most evident when addressing the topic of mnemonics. Hunter viewed mnemonics as serving mainly to facilitate memory for meaningless information, and he believed that they were not in the purview of a true academic:

> Mnemonics are mental contrivances that allow us to impose ad hoc meaning on material that is otherwise meaningless to us … since the time of ancient Greece, serious students of memory have, to say the least, been reluctant to prescribe their widespread use. Why? Because they involve us in focusing upon the kind of property, and kind of pattern, that has severely limited utility for productive thinking. (p. 163)

Importantly, Hunter associated S.'s difficulties remembering meaningful information with his use of mnemonics. Although it is not clear whether Hunter believed S.'s use of mnemonics to be a limiting factor or simply a manifestation of his lesser all-around cognitive ability, it is obvious that Hunter believed that S.'s highly perceptual encoding processes to be inferior to Aitken's form of semantic encoding. Moreover, both Hunter and Aitken adamantly denied that Aitken made use of any type of mnemonic. In Aitken's words, "Mnemonics I never use and deeply distrust. They introduce an alien perturbation into a mind, as I would have it, be pure and limpid" (Hunter, 1977, p. 163).

Despite the adamant and somewhat pompous claims to contrary, there is evidence that suggests that Aitken did in fact use mnemonic techniques to enhance his memory. Most obvious was Aitken's use of rhythm. To enhance his long-term retention of long lists, he would focus on auditory-rhythmic groupings to impose structure on the to-be-learned information. As noted in Chapter 5, the use of rhythm and/or melody can result in strong memory for large amounts material. It is also clear that Aitken used a variety of codes when processing information. His intense interest in meaning led to a thorough analysis of each stimulus. This analysis is evident in a letter from him discussing musical memory:

> Musical memory can, I am certain, be developed to a more remarkable degree than any other, for we have a metre and a rhythm, a tune,

or more than one, the harmony, the instrumental colour, a particular emotion or sequence of emotion, a meaning, however difficult to express in other terms, in the executant an auditory, a rhythmic and muscular and functional memory; and secondarily in my case, a visual image of the page which comes to rescue when all else flag; perhaps also a human interest in the composer, with whom one may identify oneself for the time that composition is being heard or performed and aesthetic interest in the form of the piece. (Hunter, 1977, p. 157)

This excerpt not only reveals the richness of his encoding but also suggests some use of mental imagery. Although Hunter does not discuss Aitken's use of mental imagery, it is clear from above that both visual and kinesthetic imagery were processed at least in terms of his memory for music. Thus, both Aitken and S. used some form of mnemonics, multiple codes, and mental imagery while processing information. It should also be noted that both men adjusted their memory strategies to accommodate especially difficult or artificial memory tasks. This suggests that both Aitken and S. refined their memory abilities with the conscious use of mnemonic techniques.

There is also an interesting similarity in the way S. and Aitken described some of their memories. Specifically, Aitken described his memory for a string of digits as "a kind of shimmer. It's as if it had left an impression. It's a funny faculty of neither seeing nor hearing. It's the kind of thing I can't describe" (Hunter, 1977, p. 160). This calls to mind S.'s description of certain memories containing "splashes" or "puffs of steam" (Luria, 1968, p. 39). For S., the "splashes" and "puffs of steam" mainly represented distractions that obscured memories, whereas Aitken's "shimmer" seems to represent a quality of certain memories. We are not suggesting that Aitken experienced synesthesia as did S.; we simply wish to point out a unique quality that was shared by both men in terms of their descriptions of memories (if not the memories themselves).

Aitken diverges most from S. in his extensive use of organization. As noted above, Aitken relied primarily on rhythmic organization to encode to-be-remembered information. His constant search for meaningful patterns would also lead to a good deal of relational processing. The question then becomes, how did Aitken offset this strong tendency toward relational processing in a way that allowed him to avoid the type of errors associated with organizational mnemonics (see Chapter 5)? First, it must be noted that there is not a good deal of empirical data related to Aitken's verbal memory that would seemingly be more subject to errors of discriminability associated with predominantly organizational strategies. Second, Aitken's memory was in no way infallible, and in terms of sheer capacity, durability, and accuracy, it was not at the level displayed by S. (Hunter, 1977). Nonetheless, Aitken's memory ability was exceptional. A partial explanation for Aitken's memory prowess in light of using mainly organizational mnemonics is his extensive use of multiple encodings. Because Aitken continually recoded to-be-learned information, the target information eventually emerged as part of a unique pattern. In addition, his broad knowledge base and quest for meaningful interpretation undoubtedly resulted in a good deal of comparison and contrast that involved both item-specific and relational processing.

The idea that Aitken's strong knowledge base contributed to his superior memory via natural distinctive processing is supported by recent research (Rawson & Van Overschelde, 2008; Van Overschelde, Rawson, Dunlosky, & Hunt, 2005), which has demonstrated that domain-specific expert memory performance can be accounted for by a combination of item-specific and relational processing. Importantly, these studies examined people with normal basic memory skills who happened to be especially knowledgeable in a particular area (NFL football). Moreover, the distinctive processing that underlay strong memory performance for these "experts" was not the result of conscious use of mnemonic techniques but a natural covariate of a well-developed knowledge base in their domain of expertise. Taking these findings into consideration, it is likely that Aitken engaged in a more or less natural form of distinctive processing at least for information in the several areas for which he was highly knowledgeable. Thus, it is likely that his conscious use of rhythmic organization was frequently complemented by the item-specific processing associated with his expert knowledge.

Similar to S., Aitken used mnemonic techniques, but his superior memory ability cannot be fully explained by the use of those techniques. It appears that Aitken's use of organizational techniques was different from that which is typical. First, Hunter's (1977) description of Aitken's use of rhythm suggests that it was used as part of a larger, more complex pattern than would be derived from a simple rhythm or melody. In this respect, it is likely that Aitken's powerful intellect played a large part in his subjective organization. Moreover, with the exception of his use of item-specific and relational processing by way of continual comparisons and contrasts, it appears that Aitken's use of mnemonics was more complicated than that which would be helpful to most learners.

☐ T. E.

Unlike S. and Aitken, T. E. and those who studied him (Gordon, Valentine, & Wilding, 1984; Wilding & Valentine, 1985) ascribed his exceptional memory skills to the use of mnemonic techniques, which he began using as a teenager. T. E. used a variety of mnemonic techniques, but his preferred method was a phonetic system nearly identical to that described in Chapter 4 (see Table 4.1). Using this method, he displayed memory accuracy for paired associates that was comparable to V. P.'s performance on a similar task, memory for number matrices that was comparable to performances by V. P. and S., and performance that exceeded that of V. P. on the Brown-Peterson test of short-term memory (see Peterson & Peterson, 1959). T. E. also displayed exceptional memory for stories, faces, and names.

The case of T. E. is especially interesting because he showed no signs of other exceptional abilities, and his basic cognitive abilities were not unusual (Gordon et al., 1984). This led Gordon et al. to conclude that T. E.'s ability was accounted for by his use of mnemonics. Moreover, the authors suggested that memory performance similar to that of T. E. could be achieved by others simply by using mnemonic techniques:

> There has been evidence to suggest that T. E.'s memory performance requires an explanation in terms of unusual basic abilities. Although he performed more accurately than "normal" subjects— indeed he even performed better than other mnemonists—all of his feats could be explained by the mnemonic "tricks" that he employed. Furthermore, there is nothing to suggest that many people could not perform memory tasks as efficiently as T. E., if they had a full knowledge of the mnemonic techniques used and were prepared to practise them to the same extent. (Gordon et al., 1984, p. 13)

The conclusion made by Gordon et al. echoes the sentiments of Ericsson and colleagues (e.g., Chase & Ericsson, 1982; Ericsson, 1985) who have argued that exceptional memory can be achieved solely through extensive practice. Although we do not necessarily endorse this claim, we do believe that the mnemonic methods used by T. E. are worthy of close examination.

As mentioned above, T. E. made extensive use of the phonetic system. However, it should be noted that T. E. often combined the phonetic system with other mnemonics in order to meet the demands of a given learning task. For example, in Gordon et al.'s (1984) Experiment 1, T. E. was required to learn numerous paired associates each composed of a trigram and a two-digit number. At testing, T. E. was provided with the trigram and asked to recall the associated number. This task was made more difficult by using only four trigrams, which were continually being repaired with different numbers, and by varying the number of intervening trials prior to recall. T. E. approached this task using a combination of the phonetic system, the story method, and a component that resembles the peg-word method. First, he converted each trigram into a word based on meaningful associations. He then converted each number to a word using the conversion prescribed by the phonetic system. The words representing each of the trigrams then served as peg words that he associated with the words representing numbers via interactive mental imagery. He then linked the interactive mental images together using the story method. Thus, this skillful combination of methods allowed T. E. to convert relatively meaningless information (trigram–number pairs) into meaningful images and then organize them in serial order within the context of a story. This is a fine example of achieving distinctive processing by combining elaboration with organization.

T. E. also combined a variation of the peg-word method and the phonetic system to remember arrays of numbers. For example, in Gordon et al.'s (1984) Experiment 3, T. E. was presented with an array of 48 numbers that was divided into eight rows. T. E. created a word and, subsequently, a mental image to represent each row using the phonetic system. He then separated the numbers composing each row into two groups of three numbers, which he again converted to words using the phonetic system. Then, using interactive mental imagery, he created a scene for each row that included images of the words representing the number groups within the row. This method afforded T. E. a good deal of flexibility at testing because the array could be easily recalled in order or by rows selected randomly by others. Clearly this method was effective as evidenced by T. E.'s perfect performance on the task. Moreover, T. E. required less study and recall time to complete this and similar tasks than did V. P. or S.

T. E. used simpler mnemonic techniques to remember stories, faces, and names. In an experiment in which the presentation rate precluded the use of formal mnemonic techniques (Wilding & Valentine, 1985, Experiment 1), T. E. outperformed control participants in memory for themes and episodes of stories by simply using mental imagery. However, as noted by Wilding and Valentine, if T. E. used only mental imagery as would most in this type of learning situation, his use of the method was obviously more efficient than the casual user's. In support of this argument, T. E. scored 4.8 standard deviations above the mean in a test of imaginal thinking (Wilding & Valentine, 1985).

T. E. also used visual mental imagery for remembering faces. However, in this case he would exaggerate a distinctive feature of the face and then superimpose this feature on his image of the face. Using this method, T. E. displayed perfect recognition for a list of 36 faces presented for 5 seconds each. Interestingly, T. E.'s exaggeration of distinctive features is similar to S.'s use of image transformation described above.

Taking all into consideration, it appears that T. E.'s exceptional memory performance resulted from skillful application of mnemonic techniques and unusually strong imaginal thinking ability. Although it is unclear whether T. E.'s superior imaginal thinking ability was the result of extensive practice with mnemonics or preceded his use of them, it is clear that his knowledge and use mnemonics contributed to his exceptional feats of memory.

□ Summary and Conclusions

The individuals discussed in this chapter represent a wide range of backgrounds, abilities, and methods. S. was a man with an unremarkable background and marked synesthesia. He displayed extremely accurate memory for long lists of letters, numbers, and words but had difficulty with meaningful materials. V. P., a man with a high IQ and expertise in a variety of languages, displayed outstanding memory for a wide variety of information. Aitken was highly intelligent and exceptionally well educated, and he engaged in an extremely analytical form of processing. He was known for his exceptional memory for numerical information, but he also displayed strong memory for a variety of other types of information. T. E. was a college graduate who developed an interest in mnemonics as a teenager and displayed exceptional memory for a variety of information including numbers, faces, and stories.

Despite some claims to the contrary, all of the individuals discussed in this chapter used at least one mnemonic technique on a regular basis. S. made extensive use of the method of loci and, more generally, interactive mental imagery. Although there are few specifics available regarding V. P.'s methods, it is believed that his technique involved a good deal of meaningful elaboration. Aitken claimed to use no mnemonic techniques, but evidence suggests that he made extensive use of rhythmic organization, multiple coding, and relational processing. T. E., unlike the others discussed, attributed all of his memory ability to the use of mnemonics. He made extensive use of the phonetic system and the story method as well as interactive mental imagery and components of the peg-word method.

It has been argued that superior memory can be achieved by virtually anyone who is willing to become well versed in mnemonic techniques (see Chase & Ericsson, 1982; Ericsson, 1985; Ericsson et al., 1980; Wilding & Valentine, 1985). However, Wilding and Valentine (2006) more recently argued that broad memory superiority such as that displayed by the individuals discussed here is unlikely to be achieved solely through mnemonic use or practice. Although we generally agree with this notion, we do believe that the use of mnemonics can significantly improve one's memory ability across a wide domain of subject areas. Moreover, we believe that highly specialized feats of memory prowess could be achieved through extensive practice with appropriate techniques. However, truly exceptional broad-based memory is likely a product of multiple factors including genetic predispositions, environmental factors, and general aptitude.

CHAPTER

Mnemonics Returns to Education

The relationship between mnemonics and education has been enduring if occasionally tempestuous. Mnemonics' place in formal education was to support the central purpose of the liberal arts curriculum, teaching effective oral communication. From the Middle Ages to the early 20th century, rhetoric was the core of the university curriculum, and mnemonics was viewed as a critical component of that curriculum. But during that period, mnemonics was sporadically criticized as ineffectual or even detrimental to true understanding and as such deserved no status in a serious education. Rote memory, the critics observed, has nothing to do with the acquisition and use of knowledge. The times have changed. Rhetoric no longer has hegemony within the university curriculum, and formal courses in mnemonics have vanished from the classroom at any level. At the same time, a pragmatic appreciation for the value of mnemonics in support of learning has given new life to selective application of mnemonic techniques in formal instruction. The upshot is a substantial body of solid research on mnemonics in classroom application.

In this chapter, we shall provide an overview of that research with two goals in mind. The first goal is to illustrate the range of applications of mnemonic techniques across disciplines and types of materials. In some cases, these applications are not surprising, such as the learning of second-language vocabulary. In other instances, the applications are rather unexpected, such as learning polynomials and problem solving in algebra.

The second goal is to highlight issues associated with the use of mnemonics in formal instruction and to cast those issues as researchable questions. For example, is it advisable to use a mnemonic requiring visual imagery in application to abstract material, given the basic research finding that imagery is of little value in memory for abstract material (Paivio, 1971)? What is the cost–benefit ratio of the difficulty of developing a mnemonic to its facilitation of learning and memory? A mnemonic technique obviously will be of no practical use if it is too difficult for students to develop. Equally obvious is that the effectiveness of a mnemonic device will hinge on the memorability of that device. One of the editors of this series mentioned to us that he learned a wonderful mnemonic in high school for the 15 reasons that the Roman Empire collapsed, but unfortunately he no longer remembers the mnemonic. Assuming the mnemonic can be remembered, it becomes important that it can be decoded. After all, it is the target of the mnemonic not the device itself that is of ultimate interest. Research is available on some of these issues, and in what follows, we selectively review that research.

☐ Areas of Application

Contemporary research on educational applications of mnemonics includes a wide range of mnemonic techniques and academic disciplines. This literature could be organized in several different ways. One could approach the task by categorizing the studies by discipline. Alternatively, one could use mnemonic devices as the organizational structure. Either of these approaches could be used to good effect, but we have chosen a third alternative. That is, one can order the goal of the mnemonic technique on a dimension of cognitive demand, anchored on one end by rote memory of single words and on the other by analogical reasoning. Our discussion will proceed along that dimension beginning with the acquisition of vocabulary and terminology. We then move on to studies on the acquisition of relationships within taxonomies and the use of these relationships in reasoning tasks. Application of mnemonic techniques to mathematics will follow that, and we finish with work on the use of mnemonics in memory for discourse.

Foreign-Language Acquisition

The road to learning an alternative language is paved with vocabulary acquisition, and for many students this is a bumpy stretch. Learning vocabulary through traditional drill methods is difficult and tedious. Consequently, any pedagogical procedure that enhances the efficiency of the process would not only be welcomed but would probably encourage more interest in the study of foreign languages. This stage is set perfectly for the application of mnemonic techniques. The basic goal is to acquire a memory for a pair of words, in this case for the meaning of a foreign word by equating it with a word in a known language. Thus, it is not surprising that we have a fair amount of information about the utility of mnemonics for foreign-vocabulary acquisition.

The favored technique, at least for research purposes, is the keyword method, which was invented in the context of foreign-vocabulary acquisition (Atkinson, 1975). Although a detailed description of the method was given in Chapter 4, a brief refresher is offered here. The technique proceeds in three stages. The first is learning the relationship between the foreign word and the keyword, which is a word in the known language that sounds like the foreign word. The second stage brings in the meaning of the foreign word through its translation in the known language. In this stage, an interactive image is formed relating the keyword to the native-language equivalent to the foreign word. For example, suppose the target to be learned is the Spanish word *perro*. Let us pick *hero* as the keyword, not only because the last syllable is similar in sound to *perro* but also because it will be easy to form an interactive image for *hero* that can be related easily to the meaning of *perro*, which is *dog*. Perhaps the image we form is of a dog on a fire truck with a medal on her collar. With the first two stages of the process mastered, the third phase is the use of the mnemonic in translation of the foreign vocabulary. The idea is that *perro* would cue *hero*, which in turn would bring the interactive image to mind and allow decoding to *dog*.

A number of studies have reported that the keyword method is more effective than rote rehearsal or simply leaving people to their own devices in learning foreign vocabulary (for reviews, see Cohen, 1987; Paivio & Desrochers, 1981). Atkinson's (1975) original development of the technique was with Russian–English translations, but since that time other languages have been used. These include German–English (Desrochers, Wieland, & Cote, 1991), Tagalog–English (Wang, Thomas, & Ouellette, 1992), and Chinese–English (Wang & Thomas, 1992). Moreover, the keyword method has been shown to be effective for second-language learning with older adults (Gruneberg & Pascoe, 1996) and children (Pressley, Levin, & Miller, 1981).

Weighing against these positive results, however, are a series of more recent negative findings (e.g., Desrochers et al., 1991; Ellis & Beaton, 1993; Wang & Thomas, 1995). One of the most thorough studies reporting no effect of the keyword method is that of van Hell and Mahn (1997). In this study, the keyword method was pitted against rote rehearsal with students who were either experienced in learning foreign language or inexperienced. Following the study session, each student was tested immediately, 2 weeks later, and again 3 weeks after the initial study session. The tests included not only a measure of accuracy of translation but also a measure of latency. Although few studies measure latency, the time taken in translation is an important index of proficiency. The surprising result was that the effectiveness of the study method varied as a function of experience with foreign languages. The experienced students performed better following rehearsal than when the keyword method was used. The inexperienced students showed no difference between the two techniques. These results held for both accuracy and latency.

Results such as those reported by van Hell and Mahn (1997) and others muddle the issue of the effectiveness of mnemonic techniques in the acquisition of foreign language. In terms of just the sheer number of studies, the balance sheet favors the use of the keyword method in the acquisition of foreign vocabulary, but the fact that the negative reports include better performance from rote rehearsal adds urgency to the need to reconcile the inconsistency among the studies. At this point, it is not clear what critical factors determine whether the keyword method will produce better or worse performance than rather standard drill techniques.

Acquisition of Terminology

Among the first requirements of introductory courses is learning new jargon. The requirements for such learning are essentially the same as those for learning foreign vocabulary: establishing a relationship between the term and its meaning. As with the acquisition of any new words, native or foreign, many students will approach this task with a standard repetition strategy, attempting to associate the new jargon with its definition through rote drill. Various mnemonic procedures could be applied to the task, but in the absence of explicit instructions to do so, few students will adopt an elaborative mnemonic strategy (Soler & Ruiz, 1996). Available research suggests that this is a mistake, and it is one that can be corrected by active intervention of instructors.

For example, the keyword method has been used with some success in introductory courses. Carney and Levin (1998a) reported a set of experiments on "neuromnemonic" materials that they developed to assist in learning terminology in introductory psychology. To test the effectiveness of their procedure, Carney and Levin compared their neuromnemonic technique with a rote repetition condition. As an example, one of the terms was *thalamus*, whose to-be-learned meaning was "relay station for incoming information." Two slightly different keyword conditions were created, in both of which a phonetically and orthographically similar keyword was associated with the novel term. In one of the keyword conditions, the experimenters supplied the images; for example, the image for *thalamus* was "Imagine a *relay* race. The first runner hands a *thermos* (*thalamus*), instead of a baton, to the next runner." In the other of these keyword conditions, the participants were instructed to generate their own image relating the meaning of the term to the keyword (*thermos*). The control comparison was a repetition condition. Shortly after the study phase, the participants were given a definition-matching task followed by a multiple-choice test that required application of the learned meaning of the terms. The results from both of these tests favored the mnemonic conditions, which themselves did not differ in effectiveness.

Carney and Levin's (1998a) use of the keyword method forced the participants to generate and elaborate the to-be-learned material, which is consistent with our discussion in Chapter 2 of the effects of generation and elaboration in basic memory research. Methods other than keyword mnemonics are capable of encouraging these processes and perhaps are more efficient for the user. To examine this possibility, Balch (2005) essentially replicated Carney and Levin's study, with the addition of two study conditions. One of these conditions required the participant, after seeing the term and its definition, to produce a paraphrase of the definition of the term, and the other condition required the participant to generate examples of the term. In both of these cases, the material would have to be subjected to some degree of elaborative and generative processing to accomplish the study tasks. When compared to the keyword method, generating examples of the term yielded comparable performance on both a test of memory for the definitions and a test of the ability to apply the term. Paraphrasing the definition, a technique frequently recommended to students, was no better than rote repetition at study.

The facilitative effect of the keyword mnemonic on the acquisition of novel terms and their definitions offers promising pedagogical support for the acquisition of new terms and their meaning. As is evident from Balch's results, other techniques can be just as effective as the keyword method, but these other techniques almost certainly will require at least as much active involvement from the student as the mnemonic and may be more difficult and error prone than a keyword mnemonic. Balch's data show that generating examples of a new concept facilitates learning of that concept, but students may have difficulty generating novel instances of unfamiliar concepts and, worse, may generate erroneous examples. On the other hand, much remains to be learned about the keyword technique in this context. In particular, we still need to know about its effectiveness over longer retention intervals and how likely it is that students will spontaneously use the method after their initial training on it.

Learning Relationships

Learning the relationships among newly acquired concepts is a more complex problem than is the acquisition of vocabulary and terms. One has to acquire individual concepts as well as the specific interconnections that constitute hierarchical relationships.

This type of learning is not an uncommon demand across the spectrum of academic disciplines from the taxonomies of science to the genealogies of history. In most of these cases, verbatim memory is required. Such a requirement is the perfect setting for application of formal mnemonics.

Some research now is available on the application of mnemonic techniques to learning of relationships among concepts. As an example of a relatively simple relational learning task, students in an eighth-grade science class were asked to learn eight minerals along with three properties of each mineral from their reading of expository text (Levin, Morrison, McGivern, Mastropieri, & Scruggs, 1986). They were instructed to use one of three study methods. In the mnemonic condition, each mineral's name was associated with a perceptually similar keyword, which in turn was related to the three properties of the mineral in an experimenter-supplied drawing. Participants in the summary condition saw the information about the minerals and their properties in graphical form while reading the text. In the free study condition, the students were told to use their own methods to learn the material. On both immediate and 3-day delayed tests for property identification, the mnemonic study condition produced the best performance on all of the measures. Moreover, the students rated the strategy as more useful than the other two study techniques. These data demonstrate that middle school students can advantageously use the keyword method to learn material from expository text.

The procedure used by Levin et al. (1986) has been extended to a much more complex learning problem involving a larger relational structure as well as specific facts embedded in that structure. Rosenheck, Levin, and Levin (1989) expanded the original procedure by teaching students botany taxonomies, hierarchical structures of plant-group names, and their specific characteristics. The material to be learned was the classification system for 16 plant groups, which was described in 12 pages of expository text. The name of each plant group and its major characteristic were included for four hierarchical levels. The participants were university students who were instructed to read through the text twice, focusing on the relationships among the groups first and then on the specific plant-group name and its characteristics on the second reading. Prior to reading the material, students were instructed to use a mnemonic strategy, a taxonomic strategy, or free study.

The mnemonic strategy entailed first learning keywords for each plant name. For example, the respective keywords for *angiosperm, dicotyledon, rubiales, sapindales,* and *rosales* were *angel, dinosaur, Rubik's (cube), sap,* and *rose,* respectively. Angiosperm is the subdivision that subsumes the class dicotyledon, which is superordinate to the orders rubiales, sapindales, and rosales. Once the keywords for each of the terms were learned, the students using the mnemonic strategy began to learn the relationships among the terms using pictorial mnemonics. An example of one such device is shown in Figure 7.1, which is designed to depict the hierarchical relationship between angiosperm and dicotyledon. On the second

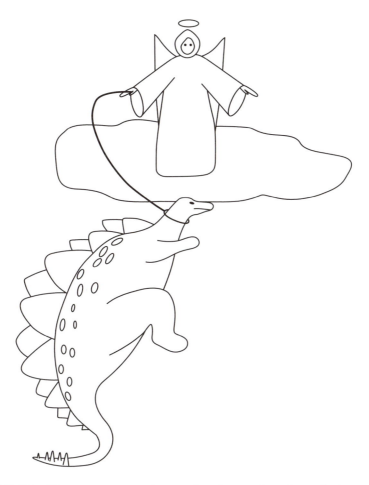

FIGURE 7.1   Picture mnemonic used to learn that dicotyledon (dinosaur) is a class of plants in the subdivision angiosperm (angel). From Rosenheck, M. B., Levin, M. E., & Levin, J. R., 1989, *Journal of Educational Psychology, 81*(2). With permission.

reading where the focus was to be on the plant's characteristic, a different picture mnemonic was used for each plant. For example, the characteristic of angiosperms was *produces flowers,* and a picture of an angel holding a bouquet of flowers illustrated it. Rather than learning keywords, the taxonomic study group started by familiarizing themselves with the plant-group names. Then on the first reading of the text, they were given a taxonomic chart to accompany the text, and on the second reading, the relevant information about the plant and its characteristic was highlighted in the text. The students in the free study group took notes if they wanted.

Later tests revealed that the mnemonic study condition produced the best memory for the specific relational and property information in the text as well as superior performance on a test that required classification of new instances to the studied categories.

This latter finding is very impressive because classification of new instances required the use of the acquired information over and above its memory. Of course, the mnemonic advantage to this task may have been due to the memory advantage for specific terms, but a follow-up study by Carney and Levin (2003) suggests this is not the case. Carney and Levin equated the original learning of the basic names but still found an advantage for their mnemonic condition on tests for the relationships within the taxonomy and their extension to new instances. Overall, this series of experiments is quite impressive in showing that the combination of the keyword method with a pictorial mnemonic facilitates acquisition of structural relationships as well as of specific facts for intervals up to 2 months. Especially important is the demonstration that the mnemonic study benefited application of the learned material to novel instances in the problem-solving test.

A final example in the domain of relational learning was chosen to illustrate the importance of matching the mnemonic to the test. In this case, students learned to identify the paintings of particular artists (Carney & Levin, 2000b). Two variations of a mnemonic study technique were contrasted with self-study on tests for retention of the original learning as well as for transfer to the identification of new paintings by the studied artists. The mnemonic study conditions began with the presentation of the artists' names along with a phonetically similar keyword. The control participants simply saw the artists' names. The next stage of study for the mnemonic conditions entailed presentation of a painting accompanied by the artist's name and keyword as well as a description of an interactive image relating the keyword and an aspect of the painting. In the detailed mnemonic condition, the image drew attention to a specific detail of that painting. In the general mnemonic condition, the image drew attention to a characteristic theme or style of the artist. The free study participants in this second stage used whatever techniques worked best for them to associate the artist's name with the painting.

Following the study session, all participants were tested immediately and then again 2 days later for their ability to match the studied paintings with the correct artists and to identify new paintings from the studied artists. On the tests for retention of the original material, the mnemonics groups outperformed the self-study group and did not differ between themselves. On the test for new paintings, however, the general mnemonics group showed the highest level of transfer from the original experience, whereas the detailed mnemonics group did not differ from the self-study group. This outcome was predicted from the basic principle of transfer-appropriate processing (Morris, Bransford, & Franks, 1977). Namely, the best study procedure is one that matches the demands of a later test; in this case, the demand to recognize a new example of a known artist's work is best met by studying general themes or technical aspects that characterize the artist's work. These results nicely illustrate the effectiveness of appropriately planned mnemonic techniques for enhancing the acquisition and transfer of newly learned information.

On the whole, relational learning, which is a ubiquitous demand in formal education, seems to benefit from mnemonic techniques. An important caveat to this generalization comes from research by Konopak and Williams (1988), who found that the mnemonic used by Levin et al. (1986) did not facilitate performance for students of below average learning ability. This result is not surprising given the complexity of the keyword method, but it is an important lead that needs to be followed.

Memory for Discourse and Loci Mnemonics

Education, both formal and informal, often is a matter of extracting, learning, and remembering important points from discursive presentations. The material may be presented in oral or written form, but in either case the goal is to learn the important points carried by the discourse. Although little research is available on the effect of mnemonics on memory for discourse, De Beni, Moe, and Cornoldi (1997) reported data showing a facilitating effect of loci mnemonics on memory for spoken discourse such as a lecture.

In this study, high school students received 6 hours of training on the use of loci mnemonics as applied to discourse. The initial instruction focused on the formation of images and was followed by a session in which 20 locations in the students' town were memorized. Next, the students were given practice in understanding discourse, selecting cue words that summarized the meaning of select portions of the passage, forming images of those cue words, and mentally placing those images at one of the town's locations. The control condition also received 6 hours of preexperimental training on the use of rehearsal to remember discourse. One week after the last training session, the students were asked to learn passages (600 to 800 words) using the method by which they were trained. Immediately following presentation of the passages, recall was requested with an emphasis on memory for the main points in their correct order. Across three experiments, the texts were varied, and recall was tested both immediately and following a delay. Memory for the discourse passage showed an impressive advantage following mnemonic training regardless of the text and retention interval. In spite of the rather heroic training session required, the benefit of the mnemonic over the traditional rehearsal strategy may offset the cost of the time in training.

A very important limitation on this conclusion was discovered by Cornoldi and De Beni (1991) and replicated in the work of De Beni et al. (1997). Namely, the loci mnemonic advantage applies only to spoken discourse. Written passages actually were better remembered following rehearsal. De Beni et al. (1997) offered an interesting explanation for this modality effect in the context of Brooks's (1967) classic study of selective interference. When two similar tasks are performed in the same modality, performance is not as efficient as when the tasks are performed in separate modalities. Brooks showed that performing a response that required locating an object in space interfered with the use of a visual image. In an analogous fashion, imagery-based mnemonics would interfere with visual processing required by reading, just as verbally based rehearsal would interfere with processing of spoken discourse.

As things stand, mnemonic training on the method of loci does seem to facilitate learning and memory for major points in spoken discourse. The procedures and results of these experiments take us back to the origins of mnemonics in rhetoric in that the mnemonic training is intense and is intended to be used on subsequently presented material. Before recommending these procedures, however, we would like to see additional programmatic research that included conditions in which notes were taken on the discourse, as normally would happen in university classrooms.

Application to Mathematics

Learning and memory of simple principles of arithmetic have long been facilitated by the use of mnemonics. A standard example is the order of arithmetic operations where a common mnemonic is My (multiply) Dear (divide) Aunt (add) Sally (subtract). Generations of students probably still remember this mnemonic, even if they rarely are asked to solve problems requiring this knowledge. It seems much less likely, however, that mnemonics would be useful for complex mathematical principles, but Machida and Carlson's (1984) study of the use of mnemonic rhymes in middle school algebra classes demonstrates otherwise.

The seventh-grade algebra classes from two different schools were followed through the module on monomials, polynomials, and problem solving that required their use as the module on equations, inequalities, and problem solving using them. All students received traditional instruction through lecture, discovery, and practice, but one class received additional mnemonic instruction with Module 1. The other class received the mnemonic instruction with Module 2. The mnemonics were verbal strings of rhymes that could be used with monomials and polynomials in Module 1 and with equalities and inequalities in Module 2. The results of posttests favored the mnemonics conditions in both modules. These results show that verbal rhymes can facilitate learning and retention of mathematics computations and problem solving.

Such a conclusion is encouraging in that analysis of errors made in mathematics problem solving has shown that students often follow incorrect algorithms rather than simply forgetting mathematical factors (Resnick, 1981), and the mnemonics developed here target retention of algorithms. Equally impressive is that the criterion performance in Machida and Carlson's (1984) study was based on new problems. Although the breadth of transfer that can be supported by this type of instruction remains to be explored, this experiment is a good beginning. Given the frustration that many students experience with algebra, the cost of creating and acquiring the mnemonics may be well worth the effort.

☐ The Benefits of Spaced Study and Practice Tests

We would be remiss if we did not mention two general strategies that are applicable to any subject matter: spaced study and practice tests. Not only are these two strategies widely applicable, they are easy to implement by either the instructor or the student. Most importantly, the effectiveness of both strategies has been demonstrated many times in controlled research environments and, increasingly, in ongoing class situations.

If to-be-learned material is studied more than once, the repeated study can follow the original study immediately or the repetition can be spaced in time. Research on the effects of spaced study can be traced all the way back to Ebbinghaus's (1885/1964) interest in distribution of practice during learning, and in their thorough review of this literature, Pashler, Rohrer, Cepeda, and Carpenter (2007) pointed out that controlled experiments have consistently shown benefits to retention of spaced study. Moreover, Pashler et al. described recent research that shows that these benefits persist over substantial retention intervals. Importantly, Pashler et al. suggested that there is regularity in the literature that recommends the optimal separation of the first and second study episode. This recommendation comes in the form of a ratio relating the time between study episodes to the time between the first study and the final test. Final test memory is optimal when study episodes are separated by 10% to 20% of the amount of time from initial study to final test. If the final test occurs 50 days after the first exposure, the optimal time for the second study would be 5 to 10 days after the first study. An instructor can take advantage of this information by testing topics more than once. The students who prepare for each test will use spaced study without knowing that they are doing so. In addition, we highly recommend that instructors educate their students about this mnemonic strategy and encourage students to implement the strategy in their study routine.

Students also should be encouraged to take advantage of the test effect. Research has consistently shown that testing memory is at least as useful and often more so than is an additional study episode for long-term retention (see Roediger & Karpicke, 2007, for a thorough review). Periodic testing allows one to assess what one knows and does not know about material, a fact emphasized by metacognitive research (Dunlosky, Serra, & Baker, 2007), but in addition, testing itself facilitates retention. Pyc and Rawson (2009) demonstrated that the long-term benefits of testing are a direct function of the difficulty in retrieving the answer. In their research, Pyc and Rawson set up conditions in which study of the to-be-learned material involved retrieving correct answers, ensuring that the correct answer was always retrieved. They varied the intervals between retrieval attempts of particular answers and found that the longer the interval between retrievals, the better the ultimate learning, even though the longer intervals made for more difficult retrieval at study.

As obvious as the advantage of self-testing may appear, Roediger and Karpicke pointed out that this simple strategy is not used consistently by many students. To the extent that the student is unaware of the advantages of testing, the instructor can encourage this mnemonic strategy as part of the study routine. Furthermore, the instructor can impose a test effect by testing a given topic more than once, for example, cumulative exams. As mentioned above, the student who studies for both tests will incur not only the benefit of spaced study but also the facilitative effect of the test effect on long-term retention. Both of these strategies are easy to use and provide tremendous mnemonic benefits for education as well as for other purposes.

☐ Remaining Research and Application Issues

The studies we have reviewed and others like them generally report positive results from the use of mnemonics in educational settings. Although some of this research has been conducted in actual courses or in settings that closely mimic those circumstances, some of the work has occurred in controlled laboratory experiments. Controlled experiments, when properly conducted, are invaluable for their yield of unambiguous data, but they usually are not performed with an eye toward the practicality of implementation in a live course situation. The upshot is that even if we know that a mnemonic device can benefit memory, the decision to use the mnemonic must weigh the benefit against potential costs.

Perhaps the most obvious costs are the time and effort required to develop, teach or learn, and apply the mnemonic. These costs are directly proportional to the complexity of the mnemonic device. Consider, for example, the procedures used by Rosenheck et al. (1989) to teach the taxonomic hierarchy for plants. Materials for this procedure are illustrated in Figure 7.1. Generation of mnemonics of this complexity and subsequent preparation of the supporting materials require substantial effort and may well be beyond the resources available to most instructors. Likewise, the time required to teach techniques such as those used by Machida and Carlson (1984) to facilitate the acquisition of principles of algebra may have to come at the expense of substantive topics, a sacrifice that is hard to justify. Basic research can inform the decision with information about reasonable expectations for benefits to learning and memory along with explicit depictions of the costs of implementing the mnemonic relative to the next best strategy.

If an instructor decides to use a mnemonic, an issue that should be given considerable thought is who should generate the mnemonic, the student or the instructor. Using only basic memory research as a guide, the answer is easy. In accord with the generation effect, self-generated material is better remembered than other-presented material (Slamecka & Graf, 1978), so one would opt for student generation. But in the actual course setting, that decision should be made in light of the complexity of the mnemonic. Obviously if the device is too challenging, the students will be unable or unwilling to use it on their own. The conservative approach would be to always use instructor-generated techniques, at least until the students are comfortable with the demands underlying the generation of a successful mnemonic.

Answering this question about who should generate the mnemonic would be easier if we had more research to guide us. Some existing research includes the source of the mnemonic as a variable, and the results are inconsistent (e.g., contrast Bloom & Lamkin, 2006; Bobrow & Bower, 1969; with Patton, D'Agaro, & Gaudette, 1991). This inconsistency probably could be eliminated through programmatic examination of the effectiveness of self- versus other-generated techniques as a function of the material and the complexity of the mnemonic.

Another important dimension on which we have conflicting information is the effect of mnemonics on long-term retention. Some research suggests that the use of mnemonics not only enhances acquisition but also facilitates longer term retention. Part of the issue here is that "longer term" rarely exceeds 1 month, whereas another part is that again the existing data are inconsistent (Bloom & Lamkin, 2006; Carney & Levin, 2000a).

Resolution of this issue is very important in the context of basic research showing that easing acquisition of new material often comes at the cost of long-term retention of that material (Bjork, 1994). At stake here is the possibility that mnemonics purchase a short-term facilitation at the expense of long-term effects of the learning. The necessary research is again a programmatic attack on the retention issue using various materials and mnemonics over a range of retention of up to at least 1 year.

We are largely ignorant of the role of individual differences in the use of mnemonics. Of most concern in the education context are measures of individual difference in cognitive abilities. What little information we have suggests that students of below average learning ability do not benefit from keyword mnemonics when learning fairly simple relational material (Konopak & Williams, 1988). This result is not terribly surprising given the complexity of the mnemonic. It also is consistent with results that we shall see in the next chapter showing that the benefit of mnemonics for cognitive rehabilitation is inversely related to the severity of the damage. Regardless, more research is needed with healthy people on the effects of individual differences in cognitive ability as a function of the particular mnemonic and the material to which it is applied.

The last issue should be the top concern. The practitioner must have a clear goal for the learner before settling on a mnemonic. This concern goes beyond selection of material to the question of exactly what the student is expected to take from that material. Verbatim memory is a relatively straightforward and obvious target for mnemonic devices, but much of education is geared to "understanding." The process of comprehension seems, on the face of it, to be antithetical to the use of mnemonics, and historically much has been made of this incompatible relationship, usually by critics of the use of mnemonics in education. There is, however, a symbiotic relationship between the psychological processes of comprehension and of memory. The idea of levels of processing (Craik & Lockhart, 1972) was premised on the notion that memory is a by-product of comprehension, and reams of experiments have demonstrated that meaningful processing of verbal material yields superior memory, even in the total absence of intent to remember. Although few direct comparisons of mnemonics based on meaningful relationships versus those based on surface-level relationships exist, we have reviewed some evidence that suggests that building meaning in the mnemonic is beneficial for later memory. Likewise, some of the evidence we have reviewed suggests that the memory advantage conveyed by the use of mnemonics served the student well in later use of the material in a new situation. In other words, memory facilitates later understanding of similar material. Thus, the recommendation is that if at all possible, mnemonics be constructed such that the device is related to the meaning of the target material.

Mnemonics in Cognitive Rehabilitation

Each year in the United States, an estimated 1.5 million people sustain a traumatic brain injury (TBI) as the result of car accidents, falls, assaults, gunshot wounds, and sports injuries, and an estimated 80,000 to 90,000 of these people will experience the onset of long-term disability *each year* (Thurman, Alverson, Dunn, Guerrero, & Sniezek, 1999). A large but unknown number of people will suffer nontraumatic brain injuries caused by brain lesions, anoxia, tumors, aneurysm, vascular malformation, and infections of the brain that are equally disabling. Add to these figures the estimated 5.3 million people with Alzheimer's disease along with 20% of the population older than age 70 afflicted with mild cognitive impairment (Alzheimer's Association, 2009). The absolute numbers will inflate with the aging of the population. Millions more people suffer from various cognitively debilitating diseases such as schizophrenia (2.2 million), epilepsy (2 million), and Parkinson's disease (1 million). However diverse the etiology and the behavioral manifestations, these various forms of injury and illness cause severe mental dysfunction, and all would benefit from effective cognitive rehabilitation. The estimates provided here are indicative of the urgent need for research and development in this field.

Almost all injuries or diseases that result in significant cognitive dysfunction involve noticeable memory losses. In some cases such as Alzheimer's disease, the memory loss is the first indication of a problem, and in other instances such as TBI, the extent of memory recovery is the barometer for prognosis and return to a productive routine. Thus, although memory is only one target of cognitive rehabilitation, it is fundamental to the entire exercise because of the importance of memory for learning and other cognitive functions. In that regard, the role of memory in cognitive rehabilitation is analogous to its role in classical rhetoric. Memory is the vehicle that carries the products of other parts of the training into behavior. Just as training in mnemonics supplemented natural memory in rhetoric, one might imagine that mnemonic training could be a useful component of cognitive rehabilitation. Indeed, we now have a good deal of information concerning the application of mnemonics to various cases of memory dysfunction, and the purpose of this chapter is to provide an overview of the issues associated with mnemonic training in service of rehabilitation. We do not attempt an exhaustive review of the published literature on the rehabilitation of memory, as several extensive reviews of that literature are available (Halligan & Wade, 2005; High, Sander, Struchen, & Hart, 2005, Parenté & Herrmann, 2003; Wilson, 2007).

☐ Goals of Cognitive Rehabilitation

Cognitive rehabilitation has been defined as a process that attempts to alleviate or ameliorate cognitive deficits suffered by people disabled by brain damage resulting from injury or disease (Wilson, 2007). Cognitive rehabilitation differs from many medical treatments in that it requires the patient to take an active role in the rehabilitation process, including assisting in the formulation and administration of the treatment plan. For example, Parenté and Stapleton (1993) reported that TBI patients learned mnemonic techniques much more readily if other patients who were more advanced in therapy actually suggested and taught the mnemonics, because the TBI patients trusted their fellow patient to empathize with their problem in a way the therapist could not. Of course, the extent of the patient's involvement in the formulation of the plan requires a level of cognitive functioning sufficient to recognize the important deficits.

Also unlike most medical treatments, programs of cognitive rehabilitation tend to be most effective when the treatment focuses holistically on social and emotional deficits as well as cognitive deficits because the goal is to allow the individuals to return to their normal environment (for examples of programs, see Parenté & Herrmann, 2003; Wilson, Herbert, & Shiel, 2003). Embedded within every program is a component devoted to memory, and it is that specific component of rehabilitation that we examine in this chapter.

The normal usage of the word *rehabilitation* connotes restoration to some former state, as in, for example, drug rehabilitation or physical rehabilitation following knee surgery. Unfortunately, such a goal for memory in the wake of serious brain injury can be unreachable. For this reason, our discussion of the literature will be guided by the distinction between *impairment* and *disability* (Glisky, 2005; Wade, 2005). As defined by the World Health Organization (2001), *impairment* is a construct designed to make sense of clinical observations, whereas *disability* is a concrete behavioral dysfunction caused by the impairment. Successful treatment of memory impairment would restore memory to its predisease or preinjury state. We know this is not possible in some cases. For example, recovery of prior memory functioning will not happen in patients with Alzheimer's disease. Evidence also indicates a similar conclusion for encephalitis (Funnel & De Mornay Davis, 1996; Wilson, Baddeley, & Kapur, 1995). The goal of treatment in such cases focuses on the disabilities caused by impairment in hopes of reducing problems of everyday life.

In contrast, some cases of posttraumatic amnesia following brain injury often show considerable *spontaneous* recovery, sometimes to complete restoration of memory. In many of these cases, the lingering memory impairment following the posttraumatic amnesia period improves following mnemonic treatment. However, a consistent finding across the literature on acquired brain injury is that the effectiveness of rehabilitation of impaired memory is inversely related to the severity of the brain damage. Memory impairment following severe brain damage does not respond to treatment (Wilson, 2005), and in the case of severe brain damage, the therapeutic focus is better placed on the resulting disabilities.

When the goal of treatment is ameliorating impaired memory, the technique used most often is drill. The rationale is that impaired memory processes can be rehabilitated by practice, much as one might rehabilitate a surgically damaged knee by using it. As we shall see, extant literature does not offer much encouragement for this approach. When the goal shifts to treating the disabilities resulting from the impairment, some headway has been made. Two techniques are quite promising here. One is teaching memory strategies targeted to particular disabilities, which are used to support either learning of new information or memory for particular activities. The second technique is the use of external mnemonic aids. A wide range of options is available to be employed here, spanning the dimension of technological sophistication.

☐ Mnemonic Techniques for Impaired Memory

The approaches to treatment outlined above vary in their targeted goals from repairing impaired memory processes to compensating behavior for those impaired processes. Of course, a program of cognitive rehabilitation might try to do both, but keeping in mind the distinction between impaired processes and disabilities resulting from the impairment, Wilson (2005) argued that there is little evidence for restoration of impaired memory processes and only scattered evidence that internal mnemonics help shore up those processes. At the same time, Wilson showed that both internal and external mnemonics are useful for treating memory-related disabilities, allowing patients to return to everyday tasks that require memory. In the following section, we shall examine some of the research that leads to such a conclusion.

Direct Training of Memory Processes

The available evidence indicates that direct training of memory is ineffective for purposes of restoring impaired memory to its normal function (e.g., Benedict, Brandt, & Bergey, 1993; Godfrey & Knight, 1985; Middleton, Lambert, & Seggar, 1991). As an example of this approach, Godfrey and Knight (1985) compared the effect of direct memory training against a control condition that engaged in activities focusing on social skills training. All participants were amnesiac alcoholics. The memory training included associate learning followed by recall tasks, picture recognition training, and practice in retaining memory for recent events. The sessions for both conditions lasted 60 minutes and occurred four times a week for 8 weeks. A battery of memory assessments was administered before the training and 4 weeks after training. Performance on the posttest showed no advantage for the memory training group. Although conclusions from this particular study are qualified by a small sample size, 6 patients in each condition, nonetheless these data are consistent with those reported by others. In most cases, direct training facilitates learning of the trained material, but the effect of training does not generalize beyond those materials. There is little evidence that impaired memory function can be restored beyond the level of initial spontaneous recovery, whether by direct training or any other means (e.g., Kapur, Glisky, & Wilson, 2002).

Teaching Memory Strategies

Another frequently used approach for treating memory impairment is teaching strategies that also increase memory in laboratory research with healthy individuals. A variety of strategies have been used including elaboration and organization, but the majority of the effort has been devoted to imagery. Richardson (1995) concluded from his review of the literature that the effects of imagery training are highly variable, and he isolated some important contributions to this variability. Perhaps most notable is that the effects of imagery training are inversely related to the severity of the memory impairment. This fact is almost certainly attributable to the difficulty of acquiring the imagery strategy. For example, more complex strategies such as the peg-word technique yield very poor outcomes even with moderate impairment. A significant problem noted by Richardson is the lack of generalization to everyday memory, which itself may be due to the failure to remember to use the strategy. On the whole, strategy training on functionally neutral material is not beneficial (Gade, 1994; Kaschel et al., 2002; Richardson, 1995).

On the other hand, strategy training has yielded positive outcomes when treating disabilities engendered by memory impairment. For example, Kaschel and colleagues (2002) compared an intense imagery training program consisting of 30 sessions over a 10-week period against the same schedule using the standard memory training the patients would have received in their therapy. Training began with exercise in generating simple images of common objects and progressed to more complex imagery of individualized tasks selected by the patients. On a follow-up test 3 months after training, the imagery group performed better than the standard treatment group, and impressively this advantage extended to everyday activities. Kaschel et al. noted the caveat that the benefits were greatest in cases of mildest impairment. Nonetheless, these data offer some encouragement for the utility of strategy training on targeted disabilities.

The success of Kaschel et al.'s procedure in obtaining generalization to everyday activities owes much to the fact that patients selected the tasks that were relevant to their lives. Indeed, internal mnemonic strategies can be used effectively by impaired patients to remember the material on which the strategy was trained, but there is little evidence of generalization beyond those materials (Rees, Marshall, Hartridge, Mackie, & Weiser, 2007). Thus any lasting benefit from strategy training must target specific aspects of behavior disabled by memory impairment. With that goal in mind, research has yielded positive results of strategy manipulations in the context of assisting new learning. This result is encouraging in that one can target a particular skill or bit of knowledge and then employ particular strategies in the acquisition of that behavior or knowledge.

One technique that has received considerable attention is the use of errorless learning. Errorless learning is engineered by designing an acquisition phase that eliminates any possibility of error. A nice example of this approach is the work of Baddeley and Wilson (1994). In this research, amnesic patients, healthy older adults, and healthy younger adults were required to learn a list of words. In one condition, the learning was by trial and error. For each word, the participants were given information of the following kind: "I am thinking of a five-letter word that begins with DE. Can you guess what the word is?" After the guess, the participant was told the word. The purpose of this condition was to induce errors in the learning trial. In a second condition, the learning trial proceeded without errors. For example, the information provided for each word was in the form of "I am thinking of a five-letter word that begins with DE, and the word is DEALT." Memory for the words in the list was best in the errorless trial for all groups, but the advantage was greatest in the amnesic group.

The errorless learning procedure has been applied with amnesic patients in situations ranging from teaching them aspects of computer technology (Glisky & Schacter, 1989) to learning their therapist's name (Wilson, Baddeley, Evans, & Shiel, 1994).

The rationale for the technique is grounded in the theoretical distinction between consciously controlled cognitive and automatic processes (Jacoby, 1991) and is applied to memory disabilities on the assumption that memory impairment is a deficit in consciously controlled processes (e.g., Cermak, Verfaellie, Butler, & Jacoby, 1993). Because errorless learning procedures rely on cues that support automatic retrieval from memory, the impaired individual is able to capitalize on previous learning in ways that would not be possible if retrieval required controlled processes (e.g., Glisky & Schacter, 1989). Moreover, errors committed during initial learning can exert automatic influences on behavior in the future, leading to perseveration of the errors. Suppressing these errors requires the opposition of the automatic influence of the previous error by consciously controlled processes, but memory impairment eliminates consciously controlled memory. Thus, errorless learning is well suited for rehabilitation of targeted behavioral disabilities.

External Mnemonic Aids

Another effective means for treating disabilities accompanying memory impairment is the use of external memory aids. External aids tend to be easier to use than internal mnemonic strategies, which may account for people's preference for external aids over strategies in their daily lives (Long et al., 1999), and most applications of external aids easily target specific disabilities for the individual. As is the case with normal memory, the aids used to assist the memory-impaired individual run the gamut from simple reminder notes to computer-controlled paging systems. The most serious obstacle to the effective use of external aids is that memory often is required. Thus, the impaired individual needs considerable support while learning to use the aid, and in some cases of technologically sophisticated aids, the complexity will exceed the ability of the impaired person.

Considerable evidence exists showing very clear and strong beneficial influence of external aids (for reviews, see Kapur et al., 2002; Sohlberg, 2005). Wilson, J. C., and Hughes (1997) reported an interesting example of a severely amnesic young man, J. C., who developed his own system of compensatory strategies. J. C. kept a diary containing extensive notes of his successes and failures in his efforts to develop effective strategies. That information was complemented by the notes maintained by J. C.'s aunt during the same period. Drawing on these resources, Wilson et al. (1997) were able to track J. C.'s progress for 10 years after his recovery from surgery for the cerebral hemorrhage that caused the amnesia. Although he was still densely amnesic after that 10-year period, he was living on his own and was completely independent. In part that success was due to the fact that his memory impairment is not accompanied by other cognitive impairments, but J. C.'s independence could not have been achieved without the strategies he developed. As described by Wilson et al. (1997), these strategies began with simple notes to himself and evolved to include aids such as a databank watch, a personal organizer to remind him of imminent appointments, and a small tape recorder on which he recorded important events as they happened so that he could review them later. Through observing his own errors, he developed the habit of keeping information he needed to remember in two separate systems. Although these mnemonic supports were not sufficient to allow him to resume his studies of law at Cambridge, J. C.'s ability to live on his own is an important example of the power of even rather simple external mnemonics to overcome the disabilities imposed even by severe amnesia.

Another low-technology intervention is the memory book. The memory book contains names and addresses as well as reminders about daily activities that the individual has designated as important but frequently forgotten. The book also has space for the individual to record events as they happen, which can be used to support later memory. Several studies have reported some benefit through the use of memory books (e.g., Donaghy & Williams, 1998; Owensworth & MacFarland, 1999). These same studies have cautioned that explicit and systematic training in the use of the memory book is required to obtain benefits.

High-tech devices are becoming much more common in rehabilitation, mirroring the trend in the general population of increased use of such devices to assist memory and organization. Some of the devices used by the nondisabled population have been tried with impaired groups. For example, Van Den Broek and colleagues (2000) provided a group of 5 brain-damaged patients with a voice-organizer, which was a simple Dictaphone-like device that allowed the patients to self-record messages. The devices with accompanying message alarm functions were effective in reducing memory failures for the specific tasks of delivering a message to another person and performing routine chores.

An increasing number of devices explicitly designed for the memory impaired are now available, and some of these have been evaluated rather carefully. Promising results have emerged from the use of paging systems specifically designed for use by memory-impaired people (see Sohlberg, 2005, for a description of various devices and their support systems). Perhaps the most thoroughly researched of these systems is NeuroPage (Hersh & Treadgold, 1994), which is a handheld device with a screen that is connected to a central computer as well as by telephone to a paging company. The scheduling of reminders is entered into the computer, and at the appropriate time the reminder is transmitted to the terminal where it is converted and sent as a radio signal to the individual user. When a reminder comes in, the device emits a visual cue and an auditory cue, and the message is displayed on the screen. Importantly, the user is requested to telephone the paging company to confirm the message, and if the user fails to do so, the message is resent. The device is controlled by one large button, making it simple for the user. Once the reminders are entered into the computer, no further human interface is required.

The NeuroPage system has been subjected to several evaluations, one of which was extensive. Wilson, Emslie, Quirk, and Evans (2001) conducted a controlled study involving over 100 brain-damaged patients, which is a large sample for research in this area. After a baseline period of 2 weeks, one group received the pager for 7 weeks. The control group members were placed on a waiting list for the pager and continued their usual therapy. After 7 weeks, the waiting group was put on the pager, and the other group was taken off. An additional 5 weeks of observation of target behaviors ensued. The percentage of target behaviors successfully completed is shown in Figure 8.1. At the initial baseline, no difference existed between the two groups, but after that point, the group that had a pager performed considerably better than the group without one.

The only real disadvantages of paging systems such as NeuroPage is that someone has to convey the scheduling information to a central

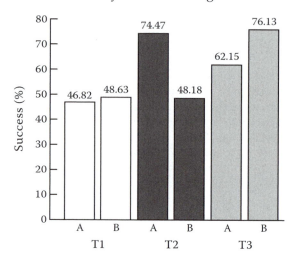

FIGURE 8.1   Percentage success rate for participants in Group A, who had the pager at T2 (Weeks 8, 9), and for Group B, who had the pager at T3 (Weeks 15, 16). T1 is baseline. From Wilson, B. A., Emslie, H. C., Quirk, K., & Evans, J., 2001, *Journal of Neurology, Neurosurgery, and Psychiatry, 70*. With permission.

computer for programming. The programming cannot be done by the individual user. Some expense also is involved, but it is very likely that the use of such systems will save health care money by enhancing the independence of impaired patients. These systems are flexible and can be adapted for use by different diagnostic groups and at different times in the recovery period for a particular group. The initial success of such technology coupled with the fact that the technology will become even more powerful and usable constitute the most promising developments to date in memory rehabilitation work.

☐ Evaluating the Effectiveness of Mnemonics in Cognitive Rehabilitation

The select sample of the literature that we have discussed is representative of what is now a fairly large number of published studies on the application of mnemonics in memory rehabilitation. We have seen that the restoration of memory processes following brain damage to their prior level of function is usually out of reach. This conclusion is not surprising because the brain structure and processes that support particular memory functions are destroyed in many cases, and nothing short of regenerating the tissue could restore the original memory processes. On the other hand, some mnemonic techniques do seem to ameliorate if not eliminate the disabilities caused by memory impairment. However, do we know enough at this point to recommend with some confidence to patients and their families that intensive mnemonic treatments will be clinically effective?

Attempts to answer this question have come in the form of systematic reviews for purposes of establishing evidence-based treatment guidelines. These reviews cover all aspects of cognitive rehabilitation, but in each case specific sections are devoted to memory rehabilitation. The most ambitious of these has been provided by Cicerone and colleagues (2000, 2005), which cover research up to 2002. Their review concludes that there is some evidence for the clinical effectiveness of training memory strategies with mildly impaired cases, a conclusion based almost entirely on the imagery training study of Kaschel et al. (2002). A strong recommendation is given for the clinical use of external assistive devices for moderate to severe impairment based on the study of NeuroPage by Wilson et al. (2001).

Rees and her colleagues (2007) provided another review that examined studies published between 1986 and 2006. Their conclusions were at least as enthusiastic as those of Cicerone et al. about the clinical value of memory training for ameliorating disabilities. Rees et al. concluded that there is strong evidence for the effectiveness of training internal memory strategies, although they did note that the duration of these effects is not known, and the strategies are effective only for mildly impaired cases. They also found strong evidence for the effectiveness of external aids with more severe cases. On the bleaker side, Rees et al. are in agreement with Wilson (2005) that there is no evidence for the effectiveness of training protocols designed to restore impaired memory processes that would justify clinical use.

A meta-analysis published by Rohling, Faust, Beverly, and Demakis (2009) provides an important quantitative evaluation for clinical use of various treatments. This analysis is especially informative because it covers the same literature reviewed by Cicerone et al., giving us a quantitative estimate of treatment effectiveness to compare with the conclusions based on the earlier qualitative analysis. Of the 258 articles reviewed by Cicerone et al. (2000, 2005), 115 contained sufficient information to be included in the meta-analysis, and of these 14 specifically targeted memory. All of the studies conformed to one of two general types of designs. Some designs were single groups of participants who were assessed on criterion measures both pre- and posttreatment. Other studies contained independent control groups that did not receive treatment thought to be effective for memory between the first and second test. Various types of control activities were used across the studies, but in all cases the outcome of interest was the improvement in the posttreatment measure for the treatment condition compared to the control condition.

The different types of designs turned out to be a very important variable for evaluating the effectiveness of memory rehabilitation. Studies using a single-group design yielded effect sizes corresponding to strong effects of memory treatment. On the other hand, independent-control-group designs resulted in very small effect sizes that were not statistically reliable. However, in the course of this analysis, an important discovery was made. Rohling et al. (2009) found that the effect size for the control condition alone was significant and of a moderate size in the independent-group design. That is, the control conditions showed significant improvement on the posttest in the absence of any effective treatment. This effect in the control condition is most likely a test effect: having taking the first test enhances performance on a second test. That the test effect occurs in these studies using amnesic individuals is a testament to the importance of automatic memory processes, but the presence of a test effect has immediate implications for the interpretation of the studies using a single-group design. In the single-group design, the treatment effect is confounded with the test effect and consequently complicates interpretation of the large treatment effect from those single-group-design experiments. If the treatment effect yielded by those studies is dismissed, the meta-analysis produced no evidence for the effectiveness of memory training. All in all, one can safely say that the support for effective mnemonic rehabilitation is much weaker following this meta-analysis than it was from the qualitative studies.

☐ Issues for Research

Performing research designed to assess the clinical effectiveness of rehabilitation is no easy task. Gaining access to and cooperation of target populations is a challenge, and the overriding goal of therapy is rarely compatible with the demands of highly controlled research. If the choice is between a perfectly designed study and no study at all, it is certain that much of the information we have about the effectiveness of treatment would not exist. At the same time, the ability to judge the effectiveness of rehabilitation is a direct function of the quality of the information available. Our overview of the literature makes clear that we need more data from well-controlled studies even though some of the criteria will be difficult to satisfy.

Among the most important considerations is an independent control group. The results of Rohling et al. (2009) dramatically emphasize the difficulty of interpreting the results from a single-group, test–retest design. The testing effect can be large and completely confounded with the treatment effect. Furthermore, researchers in this area would profit from some discussion about standardizing the activities of the control condition. As it currently stands, the content of the control group's activities is highly variable across studies, ranging from no treatment at all to the normal treatment regime of the provider. Treatment duration is equally variable and renders comparison across studies even more hazardous.

Another important consideration is the potential confounding in many studies of etiology and age. For example, a sample of brain-damaged patients that includes both TBI and stroke patients almost certainly contains this confounding because the primary cause of TBI is automobile accidents, predominantly a young person's problem, whereas the probability of stroke increases with age. This confounding can color the treatment effect because of the independent effect of age on memory.

The severity of the brain damage is a major determinant of treatment efficacy. Memory following severe brain damage appears to be impervious to attempts to restore that memory, whereas milder damage yields some benefit from memory training. In many studies, it is difficult to assess the severity of damage, and such assessment across studies is rarely possible. Indeed, Rohling et al. (2009) speculated that the differences between their recommendations and those of Cicerone et al. (2000, 2005) for the effectiveness of memory treatment may be due to this factor. That is, Rohling et al. had no metric to partial out severity in their meta-analysis, and hence they collapsed over that variable. Cicerone et al.'s more positive recommendations were based exclusively on studies using mildly impaired individuals. Again, researchers in this area would benefit enormously from some standard measure of severity of damage.

☐ Healthy Aging

We shall end the chapter on a positive note with a brief discussion of mnemonic interventions in memory decline associated with normal aging. Although the memory deficit accompanying healthy aging is qualitatively less problematic than that associated with brain injury, noticeable memory decline does occur with age. For example, a study of 1,000 participants between the ages of 35 and 80 who were tested on two occasions 5 years apart showed a rather large decline in episodic memory performance beginning around the age 55 to 60 (Rönnlund, Nyberberg, Bäckman, & Nilsson, 2005). Fortunately there now is a good bit of research available on both the basic memory processes affected by aging and controlled studies of rehabilitative techniques. Encouraging results have been reported from these later studies not only on methods that allow compensation for the memory deficit but also on approaches that appear to successfully rehabilitate the underlying memory process.

A rather substantial number of studies reporting the effects of training on older adults' episodic memory performance are available. In a meta-analysis of these studies that compared pre- and postmnemonic training performance, Verhaeghen, Marcoen, and Goossens (1992) concluded that training significantly improved performance of the trained group relative to control conditions. The mnemonic techniques entailed in the meta-analysis included method of loci, name–face learning, and organizational strategies, and the results showed that the various techniques used across the reviewed studies were equally effective. As encouraging is a report that training to generate memory strategies continued to benefit performance among older people 8 months after the training (Derwinger, Neely, & Bäckman, 2005).

Craik and his colleagues (2007) reported the results of a 12-week multimodular training program involving healthy adults 71 to 87 years old. The memory portion of the program occurred over 4 weeks and included instruction on the nature of memory and how to improve performance as well as training on internal and external memory strategies. Assessment occurred prior to training and then 3 and 6 months subsequent to training. Relative to the pretraining baseline, posttraining performance showed gains that continued to increase at the 6-month assessment. Although the authors cautioned that their results may be due to general effects of the overall training program, the findings are consistent with Derwinger et al.'s (2005) report of specific memory training benefits.

The locus of aging effects on basic memory processes has been the focus of promising research from the perspective of dual-process theory. As described earlier in this chapter, dual-process theory assumes that memory entails two qualitatively different forms of remembering: consciously controlled processes (recollection) that provide access to details of prior experience and automatic processes (familiarity) that do not access such details. Jacoby (e.g., 1999) has shown convincingly that aging has its detrimental effect on controlled processing, leaving automatic influences of the past relatively unscathed. In part this means that the automatic processes that bring inappropriate items to mind because of their familiarity are unopposed by controlled processes, leading to mistakes such as repetition errors.

On the basis of this theoretical analysis, Jennings and Jacoby (2003) developed a technique to train the use of recollection processes. They called their approach the *avoiding-repetitions* procedure. The procedure is quite simple. Participants study a list of words for later memory. A recognition test follows in which the participants say yes to the studied words and no to nonstudied words. Furthermore, they also are correctly told that some of the nonstudied words will be repeated in the test, but they should always say no to a nonstudied item. Relying on familiarity alone, the older individuals will often say yes to repeated new items. If they could recollect that the word had been shown previously in the test, familiarity would be opposed by that recollection, and they would correctly say no to these repeated lures. To train the use of recollection among the older individuals, Jennings and Jacoby used very short lags of one or two intervening items at the beginning of the test. The lags were gradually increased at a rate dependent on the individual's ability to meet a preset criterion based on younger individuals' performance. After training, the older adults showed marked improvement over their pretraining performance, now performing at a level equivalent to that of the younger adults. Moreover, the benefit persisted through a 3-month interval.

Using the theory and techniques described by Jennings and Jacoby, Toth, Daniels, and Jacoby (2005) developed a computer game called Art Dealer constructed explicitly to train recollection. The player's goal is to assemble a world-class art collection by going to 30 private art sales where the player attempts to acquire original paintings by famous artists. To buy the paintings, the player borrows money from a financier who also gives the player information about the paintings to be sold at the upcoming auction. The information is in the form of presentation of actual digitized versions of works by famous artists, which constitute the memory set for the round. After seeing the set, the player proceeds to the sale where he or she sees pictures one at a time and must decide whether to buy the picture or pass. Pictures that were not seen in the original set are, by the rules of the game, forgeries and are to be avoided. These forgeries are repeated during the course of the sale. Within this context, the avoiding-repetitions procedure described by Jennings and Jacoby is implemented. Feedback from the financier is provided following each sale, and the player can go to the "gallery" to view the collection. Financing is a part of the game in that the player occasionally may need to borrow more money from the financier but must maintain a certain balance, which is aided by sometimes selling part of the existing collection. Thus the avoiding-repetitions procedure is embedded in a play-at-home video game, but the instructions and descriptions never mention that the game is a memory training tool.

Toth et al. (2005) reported data from a study in which one group of older adults was given copies of Art Dealer and asked to play the game for 1 to 2 hours per day until the participants had completed the 30 rounds of the game. A nontreatment control group was given the same pre- and posttraining assessment as the players. The control group was carefully matched to the training group on age and other important variables. All of the training individuals completed all 30 rounds of the game, which is an impressive compliance rate for training studies. The posttraining assessment showed substantial gains for the training group members over both their own pretraining baseline and the performance of the control group. In a final interview after completing the study, all of the players rated the experience as positive and favorably endorsed the general idea of playing games to enhance cognition, saying that they would play this or similar games at home if they were shown to enhance cognitive performance.

Although preliminary in its scope, the work of Toth et al. (2005) illustrates the promise of a gaming approach to mnemonic training among healthy older people. The approach has several advantages over more traditional mnemonic training regimens. Computer games are more engaging in that people feel as if they are playing rather than working at rehabilitation. For example, 9 of the 11 players in Toth et al.'s study said they felt as if they were involved in a game not a memory test. By a similar majority, the participants said that they would play games such as Art Dealer at home if the games were known to enhance memory function. An important practical advantage is that training-by-gaming requires minimal visits to a laboratory or rehabilitation site, and the schedule of training can be determined by the individual. Finally, computer games offer an appealing and relatively inexpensive approach to maintaining and enhancing memory skills in older adults. We expect to see increasing development and deployment of computer games in service of memory rehabilitation.

☐ Summary

In this chapter we have described the goals and methods commonly used in attempts to rehabilitate memory. Interventions typically target one of two goals: restoration of basic processes to preinjury functioning or amelioration of disabilities caused by the impaired processes. With the exception of very mild impairment accompanying minor brain injury or normal aging, attempts to restore impaired processes have been unsuccessful. Treatments targeting specific disabilities have yielded positive outcomes, in some cases even allowing amnesic individuals to live on their own. Success this dramatic is rare, but mnemonic techniques designed for individual needs frequently have been shown to enhance the quality of life for both patients and caregivers. As we move forward, it will be as important to support research evaluating these techniques as it is to continue the development of the techniques themselves. As we have seen, performing research in this area is challenging, and existing work is less than perfect. Careful research on rehabilitation techniques and their effectiveness must be a high priority if we are to succeed in applying mnemonics broadly conceived to the important domain of memory impairment.

9

So, Is There a Place for Mnemonics in Contemporary Psychology?

Here at the end of our discussion of mnemonics, we think it appropriate to revisit the question raised in the title of the first chapter. Where, if at all, does the study of mnemonics belong in modern psychology? In this final chapter, we shall provide a synopsis of the book that addresses this question.

☐ Mnemonics in Basic Memory Science

The obvious home in psychology for the study of mnemonics is within the community of memory scientists. Ironically, certain basic premises of memory research are subtle obstacles for widespread acceptance of mnemonics. Chief among those is that the proper subject of memory theory is the natural operation of memory. This tension between natural memory and the artificial techniques of mnemonics is not new and, as represented in contemporary psychology, not particularly fractious or principled. On the other hand, it is true that the implicit goal of explaining natural memory does not easily incorporate artificial memory. The goal of basic science since the time of Ebbinghaus has been to explain the operation of memory, whereas the sole purpose of mnemonics is to improve memory. These goals are compatible, but they are different. For these and other reasons, very little research on mnemonics appears in the journals of basic memory research.

That said, a symbiotic relationship does exist, at least in principle, between basic memory science and mnemonics. The contribution of basic research to mnemonics is usually perceived as the more important component of the relationship. After all, carefully controlled experiments are the final authority on what does and does not affect memory. Conditions that encourage imagery, organization, and elaboration have been studied intensively, and all clearly benefit memory. These three operations, imagery, organization, and elaboration, are the basis of virtually all mnemonic devices, and, as such, one might argue that basic research has provided the foundation of mnemonics. On that view, the relationship is not symbiotic but asymmetrical, dominated by science of which mnemonics is but an application. Such a view, however, is clouded by the historical fact that imagery, organization, and elaboration were in mnemonic use long before a science of memory existed. Indeed, many contemporary scientific papers, especially on imagery, will introduce the topic by referring to classical uses of those operations in mnemonic devices.

Perhaps a better metaphor is that basic research and mnemonics are two diverging paths with the same starting point. That starting point is intuition about the operations that improve memory. Mnemonics takes the intuition as the basis for creating devices to facilitate memory, whereas basic science proceeds from the intuition to an analysis of how the benefit occurs. Both paths can contribute to validating the initial intuition. The mnemonic may not serve its purpose, or the basic research may discover that the intuitive operation is actually something else. Along the way, a symbiotic relationship can emerge for the mutual benefit of basic and applied memory science.

☐ Mnemonology

We have suggested that this interface between basic memory research and mnemonics be called *mnemonology*, which is essentially the study of processes that facilitate memory. A number of these processes have been described throughout the book, along with the basic science that validates their facilitative effect. To take just one example that we described previously, basic research has established that the joint operation of organization and elaboration, herein referred to as *distinctive processing*, facilitates memory beyond the operation of either alone. Research even has shown that it is this distinctive processing that seems to characterize the domain-specific memory advantage of experts (Rawson & van Overschelde, 2008; van Overschelde, Rawson, Dunlosky, & Hunt, 2005). No mnemonic has been intentionally developed to capitalize on this discovery, although some applications of existing devices are probably doing just that. Successful creation of a technique based on these principles would be a powerful tool. As basic memory theory progresses, mnemonology should be in the position to capitalize on new discoveries by developing techniques grounded in the basic facilitative processes.

Mnemonology also will contribute to the goals of basic research through the study of mnemonic devices, which can yield useful scientific information about the contexts in which certain variables have beneficial effects. These contexts are likely to be richer and more complex than is normally tolerated in basic research, but these more complicated situations can yield observations that stimulate research interest in a new phenomenon. For example, we reviewed a study by Balch (2005) that compared three techniques for learning the definitions of terms. Interestingly, Balch found that generating an example of each term yielded performance equivalent to that of a keyword mnemonic, both of which were better than paraphrasing the definition. Is this a reliable result? Why should generating an example of a term lead to better memory for a definition than paraphrasing that definition? Answers to these questions would contribute to our understanding of basic processes not only in memory but also in comprehension.

Memory science is the validating authority for mnemonics, and in that sense, it is the home for mnemonics in psychology. Mnemonology contributes to the basic science by identifying natural memory processes that are optimal for performance and then proceeding to apply these processes. By explicitly recognizing the different goals of the two enterprises, mnemonology can reduce the tension that historically has existed between basic science and mnemonics and foster greater effort within the scientific community to develop mnemonics into a serious applied branch of basic memory research.

☐ Mnemonology in Education

Education was the original home of mnemonics. Mnemonic techniques were taught in stand-alone courses embedded within the general rhetoric curriculum. The intent was to equip the student with useful tools to build oral argument. The utility of these techniques was not at issue; mnemonics was assumed to provide beneficial support for natural memory. This attitude has shifted over time such that now mnemonics is not offered as a course in any curriculum of which we are aware, and the effectiveness of any given technique is a matter to be demonstrated in research. Thus, it is no surprise that mnemonology has been most evident in education journals.

Research within or modeled on some education venue has become one of the most active sources of new information on mnemonics. A large number of studies ranging across ages, disciplines, and type of techniques are now available. We reviewed a sample of these studies in Chapter 7. That body of literature shows that mnemonics can be quite beneficial to learning and memory of diverse material ranging from simple vocabulary acquisition to generalization of newly acquired concepts.

Among the issues that need more research attention is the effectiveness of mnemonics for the acquisition of knowledge. Here we mean to distinguish memory and knowledge, using the widely shared assumption that knowledge is less restricted by context than is memory. In other words, knowledge transfers to contexts that are different from the acquisition context; knowledge is generalizable. A few of the studies we reviewed in Chapter 7 did report that mnemonic training was effective in the application of the acquired material to new circumstances, which begins to approximate the question we are raising. Much more of this type of research would be welcome. Another matter that deserves attention concerns the development of mnemonics that are not only effective but also user-friendly. Some of the techniques that we reviewed certainly were effective but were also very complicated. That complexity will discourage both an instructor and the student. Many issues can be identified that would benefit from further attention, making this a potentially rich area of interesting questions for both educational and psychological researchers.

☐ Mnemonics in Rehabilitation

Unlike the relationship between mnemonics and education, the use of mnemonic techniques in cognitive rehabilitation is noncontroversial. Indeed, what other choice is there for the treatment of memory loss? The literature to date on this topic is best understood in the context of a distinction between restoration of previous function and compensation for disabilities. The effect of traditional mnemonics on these two goals differs as a function of the severity of brain damage.

Traditional internal mnemonic strategies yielded successful restoration of memory function in very mild impairment, such as that associated with healthy aging. With more severe impairment, however, restoration of pretrauma functioning does not seem possible. This failure is not at all surprising. The damage inflicted on the brain by injury or disease eliminates the memory ability. In the absence of that neural substrate, no amount of training will restore original memory function. It is as if one were attempting to rehabilitate an amputated limb through exercise of the nonexistent limb. This conclusion, however, has no bearing on the utility of internal mnemonics under normal conditions and is itself subject to revision pending further research in mnemonology.

On the other hand, the literature clearly shows that mnemonic techniques are valuable therapeutic tools in service of compensatory training. A range of traditional mnemonic approaches has been used effectively to assist impaired memory with routine activities. Two additional techniques also have yielded promising outcomes. The first of these attempts to facilitate learning by essentially bypassing conscious memory demands of the acquisition task. This approach is a rare instance of convergence from Skinnerian learning theory and basic theory in memory research; the former labeled the technique *errorless learning*, and for the latter it is an example of implicit memory. The essential element of the acquisition environment is sufficient cue support to evoke the desired response in the absence of error. Subsequent test environments supply equally powerful cue support such that intentional memory of acquisition is not necessary for successful performance. Under these conditions, severely amnesic patients have been taught skills that were beyond their grasp using intentional instructional techniques. The major limitation of this approach is the narrow scope of generalization of the learning. Expanding that range of generality is an important challenge for mnemonology.

A second approach that successfully compensates for disability associated with severe brain damage is the use of external mnemonic support. These techniques range in technological sophistication from simply keeping notes to elaborate computer-controlled interventions. As a class, external mnemonics have several positive features in application to remedying disabilities. Chief among those is that most external devices are easily personalized. The particular memory demands vary widely across people, and ease of customization is a benefit for therapy. Research has shown positive results from low-technology devices such as memory books, personal organizers, and tape recorders, but one important drawback to these low-tech mnemonics is that one must remember to use them. Thus a personal organizer may be an indispensable tool for a nonimpaired person, whereas it is of limited use for a severely memory-impaired person. As the devices become more sophisticated, they are designed to overcome the disability of failing to remember to use them. This technology is exciting. It truly is artificial memory in that it supplies not only the to-be-remembered content but also the cue to access that content. Further collaboration of engineers, computer scientists, and psychologists will lead to more sophistication in these applications and a more promising course of rehabilitation for the millions of people suffering severe brain damage.

☐ Limitations on Natural Memory

Very few people seem to be impressed with their memory abilities. Complaints about forgetting far outnumber success stories of memory prowess. Such beliefs and complaints are an ironic contrast to the evidence provided by our behavior. The bulk of our repertoire is learned, and successful performance of learned behavior is the function of memory. Memory is the process that brings past experience into the present.

It is an advantageous and efficient process that confers on the species the ability to recognize experienced situations and respond to them appropriately. In this role, memory can be seen as powerful and precise. Healthy people rarely forget the things they learned such as walking, the use of language, driving, etiquette, favorite foods, and what they did yesterday and maybe even the day before. The list is functionally infinite. It would be a cruel trick of nature if something as important to survival as memory were as fickle as people seem to assume. So why does memory seem to be so difficult?

The answer to this question has its roots in the co-opting of the natural memory process for artificial purposes. Given that memory functions to make past experience available for current use, the basic requirement of memory is the ability to recognize previous experiences in the sense that an appropriate response is delivered in the current setting. This primitive memory is a component of what we now call *conditioning* or *procedural memory*. Conscious reproduction of prior experience is not necessary to this function. As Bartlett (1932) noted, "In a world of constantly changing environment, literal recall is extraordinarily unimportant" (p. 204). Retention of highly detailed information was not a selective pressure on the biological development of memory. Memory for such things as the Gettysburg Address, the 8-symbol password for your banking account, today's grocery list, or the 15 reasons the Roman Empire failed does not come naturally. Memorization of such detail is no more compatible with natural memory than is flying for human arms. Nonetheless, memory for such material is likely the standard against which we assess our ability, at least in part because the demands for detailed information seem to escalate with every advance in technology.

☐ The Value of Mnemonics

Mnemonics provides one way of coping with the day-to-day demands on memory. This fact is obvious to most people as witnessed by the widespread use of external mnemonics. Our purpose, however, is to rejuvenate an interest in and an appreciation for internal mnemonics. Part of our goal in the book has been to demonstrate that mnemonics is not exhausted by formal mnemonic systems. Rather, the domain of mnemonics extends to all memory principles known through basic research to benefit performance. With some knowledge of how memory really works, each of us can take advantage of the powerful supplement offered by mnemonic techniques.

Regardless of the context, self-generation of mnemonics tailors the device to the individual's need and ability. With a small set of basic principles and a bit of creativity, anyone can construct mnemonics that are as powerful as the formal systems. For example, a basic fact of memory is that we cannot remember that to which we did not attend. As obvious as this principle is, we often violate it and later complain about our poor memory faculties. When you are introduced to someone for the first time, your chance of remembering that person's name even in the short term goes down if you are thinking about something other than the name, which happens frequently. A simple mnemonic strategy is to intentionally use the person's name when responding to the introduction and to continue to do so if there is ensuing conversation.

The development of more complex mnemonics should take various situational factors into account. We described a number of these in Chapter 2. None of these factors are particularly complicated, but they do require knowledge of the future testing environment. For example, will I be asked to recognize or recall the information? Will I be asked for details of the context, or will I be asked for general information independent of the context? To the extent that the answers to such questions can be anticipated, the mnemonic should be tailored to that testing environment.

Another important piece of information for developing your personal mnemonic is knowledge of basic principles of memory. Some of these principles are intuitive based on our experiences with memory. For example, most people know that imagery facilitates memory. Other principles are less obvious but are easily understood once accessed. We described some of these basic principles in Chapter 3. It is our belief that people who are motivated and in possession of this minimal requisite information can facilitate their memory performance with mnemonics. We hope that our efforts in this book not only invigorate mnemonology but also encourage individuals to use mnemonics and help them do so.

NOTES

1. Thorndike studied with James as a graduate student at Harvard prior to transferring to Columbia where he completed his degree with Cattell (Boring, 1950).
2. See Tulving (1983) for a differing view of the recognition process.
3. As will be discussed later, the concept of storage is not necessary from the theoretical perspective taken here.
4. See also the 1990 film of the same name.

REFERENCES

Allen, D. I. (1970). Some effects of *advance organizers* and level of question on the learning and retention of written social studies material. *Journal of Educational Psychology, 61*, 333–339.

Alzheimer's Association (2009). 2009 Alzheimer's facts and figures. *Alzheimer's & Dementia, 5*, 234-270

Angell, J. R. (1908). *Psychology: An introductory study of the structure and function of human consciousness.* Chicago: Holt.

Atkinson, R. C. (1975). Mnemotechniques in second language learning. *American Psychologist, 30*, 821–828.

Atkinson, R. C., & Raugh, M. R. (1975). An application of the mnemonic keyword method to the acquisition of a Russian vocabulary. *Journal of Experimental Psychology: Human Learning and Memory, 1*, 126–133.

Atkinson, R. C., & Shiffrin, R. M. (1968). Human memory: A proposed system and its control processes. In K. W. Spence & J. T. Spence (Eds.), *The psychology of learning and motivation: Advances in theory and research* (Vol. 2). New York: Academic Press.

Ausubel, D. P. (1960). The use of *advance organizers* in the learning and retention of meaningful verbal material. *Journal of Educational Psychology, 51*, 267–262.

Baddeley, A. D. (2000). The episodic buffer: A new component of working memory. *Trends in Cognitive Science, 4*, 417–423.

Baddeley, A., & Wilson, B. A. (1994). When implicit learning fails: Amnesia and the problem of error elimination. *Neuropsychologia, 32*, 53–68.

Balch, W. R. (2005). Elaborations of introductory psychology terms: Effects of test performance and subjective ratings. *Teaching of Psychology, 32*, 29–34.

Barnett, J. E., Di Vesta, F. J., & Rogozinski, J. T. (1981). What is learned in note taking? *Journal of Educational Psychology, 73*, 181–192.

Bartlett, F. C. (1932). *Remembering: An experimental and social study.* Cambridge: Cambridge University Press.

Beaton, A. A., Gruneberg, M. M., Hyde, C., Shufflebottom, A., & Sykes, R. N. (2005). Facilitation of receptive and productive foreign vocabulary learning using the keyword method: The role of image quality. *Memory, 13*, 458–471.

Bellezza, F. S. (1996). Mnemonic methods to enhance storage and retrieval. In E. L. Bjork & R. A. Bjork (Eds.), *Memory* (pp. 345–380). San Diego, CA: Academic Press.

Bellezza, F. S., Six, L. S., & Phillips, D. S. (1992). A mnemonic for remembering long strings of digits. *Bulletin of the Psychonomic Society, 30*, 271–274.

Benedict, R. H. B., Brandt, J., & Bergey, G. (1993). An attempt at memory retraining in severe amnesia: An experimental single-case study. *Neuropsychological Rehabilitation, 3*, 37–51.

Bjork, R. A. (1994). Memory and metamemory considerations in the training of human beings. In J. Metcalfe & A. Shimamura (Eds.), *Metacognition: Knowing about knowing* (pp. 185–205). Cambridge, MA: MIT Press.

Blaxton, T. A. (1989). Investigating dissociations among memory measures: Support for a transfer-appropriate processing framework. *Journal of Experimental Psychology: Learning, Memory, and Cognition, 15,* 657–668.

Bloom, C. M., & Lamkin, D. M. (2006). The Olympian struggle to remember the cranial nerves: Mnemonics and student success. *Teaching of Psychology, 33,* 128–129.

Bobrow, S. A., & Bower, G. H. (1969). Comprehension and recall of sentences. *Journal of Experimental Psychology, 80,* 455–461.

Boltwood, C. E., & Blick, K. A. (1970). The delineation and application of three mnemonic techniques. *Psychonomic Science, 20,* 339–341.

Boring, E. G. (1950). *A history of experimental psychology* (2nd ed.). New York: Appleton.

Bors, D. A., & MacLeod, C. M. (1996). Individual differences in memory. In E. L. Bjork & R. A. Bjork (Eds.), *Memory* (pp. 411–441). San Diego, CA: Academic Press.

Bousefield, W. A. (1953). The occurrence of clustering in recall of randomly arranged associates. *Journal of General Psychology, 49,* 229–240.

Bower, G. H. (1970a). Analysis of a mnemonic device. *American Scientist, 58,* 496–510.

Bower, G. H. (1970b). Imagery as a relational organizer in associative memory. *Journal of Verbal Learning and Verbal Behavior, 9,* 529–533.

Bower, G. H. (1978, February). Improving memory. *Human Nature,* pp. 65–72.

Bower, G. H., & Bolton, L. S. (1969). Why are *rhymes* easy to learn? *Journal of Experimental Psychology, 82,* 453–461.

Bower, G. H., Clark, M. C., Lesgold, A. M., & Winzenz, D. (1969). Hierarchical retrieval schemes in recall of categorized word lists. *Journal of Verbal Learning and Verbal Behavior, 8,* 323–343.

Bradshaw, G. L., & Anderson, J. R. (1982). Elaborative encoding as an explanation of levels of processing. *Journal of Verbal Learning and Verbal Behavior, 21,* 165–174.

Brigham, F. J., & Brigham, M. M. (1998). Using mnemonic keywords in general music classes: Music history meets cognitive psychology. *Journal of Research and Development in Education, 31,* 205–213.

Brooks, J. O., Friedman, L., & Yesavage, J. A. (2003). Use of an external mnemonic to augment the efficacy of an internal mnemonic in older adults. *International Psychogeriatrics, 15,* 59–67.

Brooks, L. R. (1967). The suppression of visualization by reading. *Quarterly Journal of Experimental Psychology, 19,* 289–299.

Brown, A. S. (1979). Priming effects in semantic memory retrieval processes. *Journal of Experimental Psychology: Human Learning and Memory, 5,* 65–77.

Brown, E., & Deffenbacher, K. (1975). Forgotten mnemonists. *Journal of the History of the Behavioral Sciences, 11,* 342–349.

Bruce, D., & Clemons, D. M. (1982). A test of the effectiveness of the phonetic (number–consonant) mnemonic system. *Human Learning, 1,* 83–93.

Bugelski, B. R. (1968). Images as mediators in one-trial paired-associate learning: II. Self-timing in successive lists. *Journal of Experimental Psychology, 77,* 328–334.

Bugelski, B. R., Kidd, E., & Segmen, J. (1968). The image as a mediator in one-trial paired-associate learning. *Journal of Experimental Psychology, 76,* 69–73.

Buonassissi, J. V., Blick, K. A., & Kibler, J. L. (1972). Evaluation of experimenter-supplied and subject-originated descriptive-story mnemonics in a free-recall task. *Psychological Reports, 30,* 648.

Burns, D. J. (1996). The bizarre imagery effect and intention to learn. *Psychonomic Bulletin and Review, 3,* 254–257.

Campos, A., Amor, A., & Gonzalez, M. A. (2004). The importance of the keyword-generation method in keyword mnemonics. *Experimental Psychology, 51,* 125–131.

Canellopoulou, M., & Richardson, J. T. E. (1998). The role of executive function in imagery mnemonics: Evidence from multiple sclerosis. *Neuropsychologia, 36,* 1181–1188.

Carlson, L., Zimmer, J. W., & Glover, J. A. (1981). First-letter mnemonics: DAM (don't aid memory). *Journal of General Psychology, 104,* 287–292.

Carney, R. N., & Levin, J. R. (1991). Mnemonic facilitation of artists and their paintings: Effects of familiarity and correspondence. *Contemporary Educational Psychology, 16,* 154–170.

Carney, R. N., & Levin, J. R. (1994). Combining mnemonic strategies to remember who painted what when. *Contemporary Educational Psychology, 19,* 323–339.

Carney, R. N., & Levin, J. R. (1998a). Coming to terms with keyword method in introductory psychology: A neuromnemonic example. *Teaching of Psychology, 25,* 132–134.

Carney, R. N., & Levin, J. R. (1998b). Do mnemonic strategies fade as time goes by? Here's looking anew! *Contemporary Educational Psychology, 23,* 276–297.

Carney, R. N., & Levin, J. R. (2000a). Fading mnemonics: Here's looking anew, again! *Contemporary Educational Psychology, 25,* 499–508.

Carney, R. N., & Levin, J. R. (2000b). Mnemonic instruction with a focus on transfer. *Journal of Educational Psychology, 92,* 783–790.

Carney, R. N., & Levin, J. R. (2003). Promoting higher-order learning benefits by building lower-order mnemonic connections. *Applied Cognitive Psychology, 17,* 563–575.

Carruthers, M. J. (1990). *The book of memory: A study of memory in medieval culture.* New York: Cambridge University Press.

Carruthers, M. J. (2002). The Hugh of St. Victor, the three best memory aids for learning history. In M. J. Carruthers & J. M. Ziolkowski (Eds.), *The medieval craft of memory: An anthology of texts and pictures* (pp. 32–40). Philadelphia: University of Pennsylvania Press.

Cavanaugh, J. C., Grady, J. G., & Perlmutter, M. (1983). Forgetting and use of memory aids in 20 to 70 year olds' everyday life. *International Journal of Aging and Human Development, 17,* 113–121.

Cermak, L. S., Verfaellie, M., Butler, T., & Jacoby, L. L. (1993). Fluency versus conscious recollection in the word completion performance of amnesic patients. *Brain and Cognition, 20,* 367–377.

Chase, W. G., & Ericsson, K. A. (1982). Skill and working memory. In G. H. Bower (Ed.), *The psychology of learning and motivation* (Vol. 16, pp. 1–58). New York: Academic Press.

Cicerone, K. D., Dahlberg, C., Kalmar, K., Langenbahn, D. M., Malec, J. F., Berquist, T. F., et al. (2000). Evidence-based cognitive rehabilitation: Recommendations for clinical practice. *Archives of Physical Medicine and Rehabilitation, 81,* 1596–1615.

Cicerone, K. D., Dahlberg, C., Malec, J. F., Langenbahn, D. M., Felicetti, T., Kneipp, S., et al. (2005). Evidence-based cognitive rehabilitation: Updated review of the literature from 1998 through 2002. *Archives of Physical Medicine and Rehabilitation, 86,* 1681–1692.

Cimbalo, R. S., Clark, D., & Matayev, A. I. (2003). Relating sensation seeking and the von Restorff isolation effect. *Psychological Reports, 92,* 1287–1294.

Clark, L. V. (1960). Effect of mental practice on the development of a certain motor skill. *Research Quarterly, 31,* 560–569.

Cohen, A. D. (1987). The use of verbal and imagery mnemonics in second language vocabulary learning. *Studies in Second Language Acquisition, 9,* 43–62.

Cohen, B. H. (1963). Recall of categorized word lists. *Journal of Experimental Psychology, 66,* 227–234.

Colvin, S. S. (1911). *The learning process.* New York: Macmillan.

Corkill, A. J. (1992). *Advance organizers*: Facilitators of recall. *Educational Psychology Review, 4,* 33–67.

Corkill, A. J., Bruning, R. H., & Glover, J. A. (1988). *Advance organizers*: Concrete versus abstract. *Journal of Educational Research, 82,* 76–81.

Corkill, A. J., Glover, J. A., Bruning, R. H., & Krug, D. (1988). *Advance organizers*: Retrieval context hypotheses. *Journal of Educational Psychology, 80,* 304–311.

Cornoldi, C., & De Beni, R. (1991). Memory for discourse: Loci mnemonics and the oral presentation effect. *Applied Cognitive Psychology, 5,* 511–518.

Costa, P. T., & McCrae, R. R. (1976). Age differences in personality structure: A cluster analytic approach. *Journal of Gerontology, 31,* 564–570.

Couliano, I. P. (1987). *Eros and magic in the Renaissance.* Chicago: University of Chicago Press.

Craik, F. I. M. (2006). Distinctiveness and memory: Comments and a point a view. In R. R. Hunt & J. B. Worthen (Eds.), *Distinctiveness and memory* (pp. 425–442). New York: Oxford University Press.

Craik, F. I. M., & Lockhart, R. S. (1972). Levels of processing: A framework for memory research. *Journal of Verbal Learning and Verbal Memory, 11,* 671–684.

Craik, F. I. M., & Tulving, E. (1975). Depth of processing and the retention of words in episodic memory. *Journal of Experimental Psychology: General, 104,* 268–294.

Craik, F. I. M., Winocur, G., Heather, P., Malcolm, A. B., Edwards, M., Bridges, K., et al. (2007). Cognitive rehabilitation in the elderly: Effects on memory. *Journal of the International Neurological Society, 13,* 132–142.

Crowder, R. G. (1989). Imagery for musical timbre. *Journal of Experimental Psychology: Human Perception and Performance, 15,* 472–478.

Cundus, M. M., Marshall, K. J., & Miller, S. R. (1986). Effects of the keyword mnemonic strategy on vocabulary acquisition and maintenance by learning disabled children. *Journal of Learning Disabilities, 19,* 609–613.

De Beni, R., & Cornoldi, C. (1988). Does repeated use of loci create interference? *Perceptual and Motor Skills, 67,* 415–418.

De Beni, R., Moe, A., & Cornoldi, C. (1997). Learning from texts or lectures: Loci mnemonics can interfere with reading but not with listening. *European Journal of Experimental Psychology, 9,* 401–415.

De Chardin, P. T. (1959). *The phenomenon of man.* New York: Harper & Brothers Publishers.

D'Errico, F. (2001). Memories out of mind: The archeology of the oldest memory systems. In A. Nowell (Ed.), *In the mind's eye: Multidisciplinary approaches to the evolution of human cognition*. Ann Arbor, MI: International Monographs in Prehistory.

Derwinger, A., Neely, A. S., & Bäckman, L. (2005). Design your own memory strategies! Self-generated strategy training versus mnemonic training in old age: An 8-month follow-up. *Neuropsychological Rehabilitation*, *15*, 37–54.

Desrochers, A., Wieland, L. D., & Cote, M. (1991). Instructional effects in the use of the mnemonic keyword method for learning German nouns and their grammatical gender. *Applied Cognitive Psychology*, *5*, 19–36.

Donaghy, S., & Williams, W. (1998). A new protocol for training severely impaired patients in the usage of memory journals. *Brain Injury*, *15*, 333–347.

Dretzke, B. J. (1993). Effects of pictorial mnemonic strategy usage on prose recall of young, middle-aged, and older adults. *Educational Gerontology*, *19*, 489–502.

Drevenstedt, J., & Bellezza, F. S. (1993). Memory for self-generated narration in the elderly. *Psychology and Aging*, *8*, 187–196.

Dunlosky, J., Serra, M. J., & Baker, J. M. (2007). Metamemory applied. In F. Durso, R. S. Nickerson, S. T. Dumais, S. Lewandowsky, & T. J. Perfect (Eds.), *Handbook of applied cognition* (2nd ed., pp. 137–162). New York: Wiley.

Eagle, S. P. (Producer), Woolf, J. (Producer), & Huston, J. (Director). (1951). *The African queen* [Motion picture]. United States: United Artists.

Ebbinghaus, H. (1964). In H. A. Ruger & C. E. Bussenius (Trans.), *On memory: A contribution to experimental psychology*. New York: Dover. (Original work published 1885)

Einstein, G. O., & Hunt, R. R. (1980). Levels of processing and organization: Additive effects of individual-item and relational processing. *Journal of Experimental Psychology: Human Learning and Memory*, *6*, 588–598.

Elliot, J. L., & Gentile, J. R. (1986). The efficacy of a mnemonic technique for learning disabled and nondisabled adolescents. *Journal of Learning Disabilities*, *19*, 237–241.

Ellis, N. C., & Beaton, A. (1993). Factors affecting the learning of foreign language vocabulary: Imagery keyword mediators and phonological short-tem memory. *The Quarterly Journal of Experimental Psychology*, *46A*, 533–558.

Engel, W. E. (1991). Mnemonic criticism and Renaissance literature: A manifesto. *Connotations*, *1*, 12–33.

Engel, W. E. (1997). Patterns of recollections in Montaigne and Melville. *Connotations*, *3*, 332–354.

Engelkamp, J. (1995). Visual imagery and enactment of actions in memory. *British Journal of Psychology*, *86*, 227–240.

Engelkamp, J. (1998). *Memory for actions*. Hove, England: Psychology Press.

Engelkamp, J., & Dehn, D. M. (2000). Item and order information in subject-performed tasks and experimenter-performed tasks. *Journal of Experimental Psychology: Learning, Memory, and Cognition*, *26*, 671–682.

Epstein, W., Rock, I., & Zuckerman, C. B. (1960). Meaning and familiarity in associative learning. *Psychological Monographs*, *74*(4, Whole No. 491).

Ericsson, K. A. (1985). Memory skill. *Canadian Journal of Psychology*, *39*, 188–231.

Ericsson, K. A., Chase, W. G., & Falloon, S. (1980). Acquisition of memory skill. *Science*, *208*, 1181–1182.

Farah, J. M., & Smith, A. F. (1983). Perceptual interference and facilitation with auditory imagery. *Perception and Psychophysics, 33,* 475–478.

Fentress, J., & Wickham, C. (1992). *Social memory.* Oxford, UK: Blackwell.

Finkel, S. I., & Yesavage, J. A. (1989). Learning mnemonics: A preliminary evaluation of a computer-aided instruction package for the elderly. *Experimental Aging Research, 15,* 199–201.

Funnel, E., & De Mornay Davies, P. (1996). JBR: A reassessment of concept familiarity and a category specific disorder for living things. *Neurocase, 2,* 461–474.

Gade, A. (1994). Imagery as an aid in amnesia patients: Effects of amnesia subtypes and severity. In M. J. Riddoch & G. W. Humphreys (Eds.), *Cognitive neuropsychology and cognitive rehabilitation* (pp. 571–589). Hillsdale, NJ: Lawrence Erlbaum.

Glidden, L. M. (1983). Semantic processing can facilitate free recall in mildly retarded adolescents. *Journal of Experimental Child Psychology, 36,* 510–532.

Glisky, E. L. (2005). Can memory impairment be effectively treated? In P. W. Halligan & D. T. Wade (Eds.), *The effectiveness of rehabilitation for cognitive deficits* (pp. 135–142). Oxford, UK: Oxford University Press.

Glisky, E. L., & Schacter, D. L. (1989). Extending the limits of complex learning in organic amnesia: Training computer related work. *Neuropsychologia, 27,* 107–120.

Glover, J. A., Krug, D., Dietzer, M., & George, B. W. (1990). *"Advance" advance organizers. Bulletin of the Psychonomic Society, 28,* 4–6.

Godfrey, H., & Knight, R. (1985). Cognitive rehabilitation of memory functioning in amnesic alcoholics. *Journal of Consulting and Clinical Psychology, 43,* 555–557.

Gordon, P., Valentine, E., & Wilding, J. (1984). One man's memory: A study of a mnemonist. *British Journal of Psychology, 75,* 1–14.

Graf, P. (1982). The memorial consequences of generation and transformation. *Journal of Verbal Learning and Verbal Behavior, 21,* 539–548.

Gratzinger, P., Sheikh, J. I., Friedman, L., & Yesavage, J. A. (1990). Cognitive interventions to improve face-name recall. *Developmental Psychology, 26,* 889–893.

Grey, R. (1730). *Memoria technica: A new method of artificial memory.* London: Charles King.

Griffith, D., & Actkinson, T. R. (1978). Mental aptitude and mnemonic enhancement. *Bulletin of the Psychonomic Society, 12,* 347–348.

Gruneberg, M. M. (1973). The role of memorization techniques in finals examination preparation: A study of psychology students. *Educational Research, 15,* 134–139.

Gruneberg, M. M., & Pascoe, K. (1996). The effectiveness of the keyword method for receptive and productive foreign vocabulary learning in the elderly. *Contemporary Educational Psychology, 21,* 102–109.

Halligan, P. W., & Wade, D. T. (2005). *The effectiveness of rehabilitation for cognitive deficits.* Oxford, UK: Oxford University Press.

Hay, J. F., & Jacoby, L. L. (1996). Separating habit and recollection: Memory slips, process dissociations, and probability matching. *Journal of Experimental Psychology: Learning, Memory, and Cognition, 22,* 1323–1335.

Hayes, D. S., Chemelski, B. E., & Palmer, M. (1982). Nursery *rhymes* and prose passages: Preschoolers' liking and short-term retention of story events. *Developmental Psychology, 18,* 49–56.

Henshel, R. L. (1980). The purposes of laboratory experimentation and the virtues of deliberate artificiality. *Journal of Experimental Social Psychology, 16,* 466–478.

Herrmann, D. J. (1987). Task appropriateness of mnemonic techniques. *Perceptual and Motor Skills, 64,* 171–178.

Herrmann, D. J., Geisler, F. V., & Atkinson, R. C. (1973). The serial position function for lists learned by a narrative-story mnemonic. *Bulletin of the Psychonomic Society, 2,* 377–378.

Hersh, N. & Treadgold, L. (1994). NeuroPage: The rehabilitation of dysfunction by prosthetic memory and cuing. *NeuroRehabilitation, 4,* 187-197.

Higbee, K. L. (1997). Novices, apprentices, and mnemonists: Acquiring expertise with the phonetic mnemonic. *Applied Cognitive Psychology, 11,* 147–161.

High, W. M., Sander, A. M., Struchen, M. A., & Hart, K. A. (2005). *Rehabilitation for traumatic brain injury.* New York: Oxford University Press.

Hill, D. S. (1918). An experiment with an automatic mnemonic system. *Psychological Bulletin, 15,* 99–103.

Hill, R. D., Allen, C., & McWhorter, P. (1991). Stories as a mnemonic aid for older learners. *Psychology and Aging, 6,* 484–486.

Hunt, E., & Love, T. (1972). How good can memory be? In A. W. Melton & E. Martin (Eds.), *Coding processes in human memory* (pp. 237–250). New York: Wiley.

Hunt, R. R. (2006). The concept of distinctiveness in memory research. In R. R. Hunt & J. B. Worthen (Eds.), *Distinctiveness and memory* (pp. 3–25). New York: Oxford University Press.

Hunt, R. R. (2008). Coding processes. In H. L. Roediger, III (Ed.), *Cognitive psychology of memory.* Vol. 2 of *Learning and memory: A comprehensive reference,* 4 vols. (J. Byrne, Ed.). Oxford, UK: Elsevier.

Hunt, R. R., & Einstein, G. O. (1981). Relational and item-specific processing in memory. *Journal of Verbal Learning and Verbal Behavior, 20,* 497–514.

Hunt, R. R., & Marschark, M. (1987). Yet another picture of imagery: The role of shared and distinctive information in memory. In M. Pressley & M. McDaniel (Eds.), *Imaginal and mnemonic processes.* Berlin: Springer-Verlag.

Hunt, R. R., & McDaniel, M. A. (1993). The enigma of organization and distinctiveness. *Journal of Memory and Language, 32,* 421–445.

Hunt, R. R., & Smith, R. E. (1996). Accessing the particular from the general: The power of distinctiveness in the context of organization. *Memory and Cognition, 24,* 217–225.

Hunter, I. M. L. (1977). An exceptional memory. *British Journal of Psychology, 68,* 155–164.

Hyde, T. S., & Jenkins, J. J. (1969). Differential effects of incidental tasks on the organization of recall of a list of highly associated words. *Journal of Experimental Psychology, 82,* 472-481.

Hyde, T. S., & Jenkins, J. J. (1973). Recall for words as a function of semantic, graphic, and syntactic orienting tasks. *Journal of Verbal Learning and Verbal Behavior, 12,* 471–480.

Iaccino, J., & Byrne, J. (1989). Mental layouts of concealed objects as a function of imagery type and experimental conditions. *Bulletin of the Psychonomic Society, 27,* 402–404.

Intons-Peterson, M. J. (1992). Components of auditory imagery. In D. Reisberg (Ed.), *Auditory imagery* (pp. 45–71). Hillsdale, NJ: Lawrence Erlbaum.

Intons-Peterson, M. J., & Fournier, J. (1986). External and internal memory aids: When and how often do we use them? *Journal of Experimental Psychology: General, 115,* 267–280.

Ironsmith, M., & Lutz, J. (1996). The effects of bizarreness and self-generation on mnemonic imagery. *Journal of Mental Imagery, 20,* 113–126.

Jacoby, L. L. (1983). Remembering the data: Analyzing interactive processes in reading. *Journal of Verbal Learning and Verbal Behavior, 22,* 485–508.

Jacoby, L. L. (1991). A process dissociation framework: Separating automatic from intentional uses of memory. *Journal of Memory and Language, 30,* 513–541.

Jacoby, L. L. (1999). Ironic effects of repetition: Measuring age-related differences in repetition. *Journal of Experimental Psychology: Learning, Memory, and Cognition, 25,* 3–22.

Jacoby, L. L., & Whitehouse, K. (1989). An illusion of memory: False recognition influenced by unconscious perception. *Journal of Experimental Psychology: General, 118,* 126–135.

James, W. (1890). *The principles of psychology.* New York: Holt.

Jamieson, D. G., & Schimpf, M. G. (1980). Self-generated images are more effective mnemonics. *Journal of Mental Imagery, 4,* 25–33.

Javawardhana, B. (1997). Free recall in the incidental learning paradigm by adults with and without severe learning difficulties. *British Journal of Developmental Disabilities, 43,* 108–121.

Jennings, J. M., & Jacoby, L. L. (2003). Improving memory in older adults: Training recollection. *Cognitive Neurorehabilitation, 13,* 417–440.

Johnson, J. L., & Hayes, D. S. (1987). Preschool children's retention of rhyming and nonrhyming text: Paraphrase and rote recitation measures. *Journal of Applied Developmental Psychology, 8,* 317–327.

Kapur, N., Glisky, E. L., & Wilson, B. A. (2002). External memory aids and computers in memory rehabilitation. In A. D. Baddeley, M. D. Koppelman, & B. A. Wilson (Eds.), *Handbook of memory disorders* (2nd ed., pp. 757–783). Chichester: John Wiley.

Kaschel, R., Della Sala, S., Cantagallo, A., Fahlböck, A., Laaksonen, R., & Kazen, M. (2002). Imagery mnemonics for the rehabilitation of memory: A randomized group controlled trial. *Neuropsychological Rehabilitation, 12,* 127–153.

Keenan, J. M. (1983). Qualifications and clarifications of images of *concealed objects*: A reply to Kerr and Neisser. *Journal of Experimental Psychology: Learning, Memory, and Cognition, 9,* 220–230.

Keenan, J. M., & Moore, R. E. (1979). Memory for images of concealed objects: A reexamination of Neisser and Kerr. *Journal of Experimental Psychology: Learning, Memory, and Cognition, 5,* 374–385.

Kerr, N. H., & Neisser, U. (1983). Mental images of concealed objects. *Journal of Experimental Psychology: Learning, Memory, and Cognition, 9,* 212–221.

Kerr, N. H., & Winograd, E. (1982). Effects of contextual elaboration on face recognition. *Memory and Cognition, 10,* 603–609.

Khan, M., & Paivio, A. (1988). Memory for schematic and categorical information: A replication and extension of Rabinowitz and Mandler (1983). *Journal of Experimental Psychology: Learning, Memory, and Cognition, 14,* 558–561.

Kilgour, A. R., Jakobson, L. S., & Cuddy, L. L. (2000). Music training and rate of presentation as mediators of text and song recall. *Memory and Cognition, 28,* 700–710.

Kinneavy, J. L. (1990). Contemporary rhetoric. In W. B. Horner (Ed.), *The present state of scholarship in historical and contemporary rhetoric.* Columbia: University of Missouri Press.

Kolers, P. A. (1979). A pattern analyzing basis of recognition. In L. S. Cermak & F. I. M. Craik (Eds.), *Levels of processing in human memory* (pp. 363–384). Hillsdale, NJ: Lawrence Erlbaum.

Kolers, P. A., & Perkins, D. N. (1975). Spatial and ordinal components of form perception and literacy. *Cognitive Psychology, 7*, 228–267.

Konopak, B. C., & Williams, N. L. (1988). Eighth graders' use of mnemonic imagery in recalling science content information. *Reading Psychology: An International Quarterly, 9*, 232–250.

Kovar, S. K., & Van Pelt, C. (1991). Using first-letter mnemonic to improve basketball set-shot. *Perceptual and Motor Skills, 72*, 1383–1390.

Krinsky, R., & Krinsky, S. G. (1994). The peg-word mnemonic immediate but not long-term memory in fifth-grade children. *Contemporary Educational Psychology, 19*, 217–229.

Krinsky, R., & Krinsky, S. G. (1996). Pegword mnemonic instruction: Retrieval times and long-term memory performance among fifth-grade children. *Contemporary Educational Psychology, 21*, 193–207.

Kroll, N. E. A., & Tu, S. F. (1988). The bizarre mnemonic. *Psychological Research/Psychologische Forschung, 50*, 28–37.

Kubler-Ross, E. (1969). *On death and dying*. New York: Simon & Schuster.

Kuo, M. L. A., & Hooper, S. (2004). The effects of visual and verbal coding mnemonics on learning Chinese characters in computer-based instruction. *Educational Technology Research and Development, 52*, 23–38.

Kyllonen, P. C., Tirre, W. C., & Christal, R. E. (1991). Knowledge and processing speed as determinants of associative learning. *Journal of Experimental Psychology: General, 120*, 57–79.

Lachman, R., Lachman, J., & Butterfield, E. C. (1979). *Cognitive psychology and information processing: An introduction*. Hillsdale, NJ: Lawrence Erlbaum.

Lang, V. A. (1995). Relative association, interactiveness, and the bizarre imagery effect. *American Journal of Psychology, 108*, 13–35.

Langan-Fox, J., Platania-Phung, C., & Waycott, J. (2006). Effects of *advance organizers*, mental models and abilities on task and recall performance using a mobile phone network. *Applied Cognitive Psychology, 20*, 1143–1165.

Leopold, A. (1949). *A Sand County almanac*. New York: Oxford University Press.

Levin, J. R., Levin, M. E., Glasman, L. D., & Nordwall, M. B. (1992). Mnemonic vocabulary instruction: Additional effectiveness evidence. *Contemporary Educational Psychology, 17*, 156–174.

Levin, J. R., Morrison, C. R., McGivern, J. E., Mastropieri, M. A., & Scruggs, T. E. (1986). Mnemonic facilitation of text-embedded science facts. *American Educational Research Journal, 23*, 489–506.

Lewis, M. Q. (1971). Categorized lists and cued recall. *Journal of Experimental Psychology, 87*, 129–131.

Liberty, C., & Ornstein, P. A. (1973). Age differences in organization and recall: The effects of training categorization. *Journal of Experimental Child Psychology, 15*, 169–186.

Loftus, E. F. (1979). *Eyewitness testimony*. Cambridge, MA: Harvard University Press.

Loftus, E. F. (1993). The reality of repressed memories. *American Psychologist, 48*, 518–537.

Long, T. E., Cameron, K. A., Harju, B. L., et al. (1999). Women and middle-aged individuals report using more prospective memory aids. *Psychological Reports, 85,* 1139–1153.

Lorayne, H. (1957). *How to develop a super-power memory.* Hollywood, FL: Fell.

Luria, A. R. (1968). *The mind of a mnemonist.* New York: Basic Books.

Machida, K., & Carlson, J. (1984). Effects of verbal mediation strategy on cognitive processes in mathematics learning. *Journal of Educational Psychology, 76,* 1382–1385.

Manning, B. A., & Bruning, R. H. (1975). Interactive effects of *mnemonic* techniques and word-list characteristics. *Psychological Reports, 36,* 727–736.

Marschark, M., & Hunt, R. R. (1989). A re-examination of the role of imagery in learning and memory. *Journal of Experimental Psychology: Learning, Memory and Cognition, 15,* 710–720.

Marshall, P. H., Nau, K., & Chandler, C. K. (1979). A structural analysis of common and bizarre visual mediators. *Bulletin of the Psychonomic Society, 14,* 103–105.

Massen, C., & Vaterrodt-Plunnecke, B. (2006). The role of proactive interference in mnemonic techniques. *Memory, 14,* 189–196.

Mastropieri, M. A., Scruggs, T. E., & Fulk, B. M. (1990). Teaching abstract vocabulary with the keyword method: Effects on recall and comprehension. *Journal of Learning Disabilities, 23,* 92–96.

May, J. E., & Clayton, K. N. (1973). Imaginal processes during the attempt to recall names. *Journal of Verbal Learning and Verbal Behavior, 12,* 683–688.

Mayer, R. E. (2003). Memory and information processes. In W. M. Reynolds & G. E. Miller (Eds.), *Handbook of psychology: Educational psychology,* Vol. 7, pp. 47-57. Hoboken, NJ: John Wiley and Sons.

McAllister, H. A., Bearden, J. N., Kohlmaier, J. R., & Warner, M. D. (1997). Computerized mug books: Does adding multimedia help? *Journal of Applied Psychology, 82,* 688–698.

McDaniel, M. A., DeLosh, E. L., & Merritt, P. S. (2000). Order information and retrieval distinctiveness: Recall of common versus bizarre material. *Journal of Experimental Psychology: Learning, Memory, and Cognition, 26,* 1045–1056.

McDaniel, M. A., & Einstein, G. O. (1986). Bizarreness as an effective memory aid: The importance of distinctiveness. *Journal of Experimental Psychology: Learning, Memory, and Cognition, 12,* 54–65.

McDaniel, M. A., & Einstein, G. O. (1993). The importance of cue familiarity and cue distinctiveness in prospective memory. *Memory, 1,* 23–41.

McDaniel, M. A., Einstein, G. O., DeLosh, E. L., May, C. P., & Brady, P. (1995). The bizarreness effect: It's not surprising, it's complex. *Journal of Experimental Psychology: Learning, Memory, and Cognition, 21,* 422–435.

McGeoch, J. A., & McDonald, W. T. (1931). Meaningful relation and retroactive inhibition. *American Journal of Psychology, 43,* 579–588.

McKinlay, W. W. (1992). Achieving generalization in memory training. *Brain Injury, 6,* 107–108.

Merriam-Webster Collegiate Dictionary. (2007). Springfield, MA: Merriam-Webster.

Middleton, D. K., Lambert, M. J., & Seggar, L. B. (1991). Neuropsychological rehabilitation: Microcomputer assisted treatment of brain-injured adults. *Perceptual and Motor Skills, 72,* 527–530.

Miller, G. A. (1956). The magical number seven plus or minus two: Some limits on our capacity for processing information. *Psychological Review, 63,* 81–97.

Moe, A., & De Beni, R. (2004). Studying passages with the loci method: Are subject-generated more effective than experimenter-supplied loci pathways? *Journal of Mental Imagery, 28*, 75–86.

Moe, A., & De Beni, R. (2005). Stressing the efficacy of the loci method: Oral presentation and the subject-generation of the loci pathway with expository passages. *Applied Cognitive Psychology, 19*, 95–106.

Mohr, G., Engelkamp, J., & Zimmer, H. D. (1989). Recall and recognition of self-performed acts. *Psychological Research/Psychologische Forschung, 51*, 181–187.

Morris, C. D., Bransford, J. D., & Franks, J. J. (1977). Levels of processing versus test-appropriate strategies. *Journal of Verbal Learning and Verbal Behavior, 16*, 519–533.

Morris, P. E., & Greer, P. J. (1983). The effectiveness of the *phonetic mnemonic* system. *Human Learning: Journal of Practical Research and Applications, 3*, 137–142.

Morris, P. E., & Reid, R. L. (1970). The repeated use of mnemonic imagery. *Psychonomic Science, 20*, 337–338.

Moss, B. J., Worthen, J. B., Haydel, L. A., Mac Mahon, B. D., & Savoy, S. C. (2008). Relationships between personality variables and bizarreness effects in free recall. *American Journal of Psychology, 121*, 175–188.

Mumford, C., & Hall, C. (1985). Effects of internal and external imagery on performing figures in figure skating. *Journal of Applied Sport Psychology, 10*, 171–177.

Murphy, S. M. (1990). Models of imagery in sport psychology: A review. *Journal of Mental Imagery, 14*, 153–172.

Nakamura, G. V., Kleiber, B. A., & Kim, K. (1992). Categories, propositional representations, and schemas: Test of a structural hypothesis. *American Journal of Psychology, 105*, 575–590.

National Institute on Aging (1998). NIA's progress report on Alzheimer's disease.

Neisser, U., & Kerr, N. (1973). Spatial and mnemonic properties of visual images. *Cognitive Psychology, 5*, 138–150.

O'Brien, E. J., & Wolford, C. R. (1982). Effect of delay in testing on retention of plausible versus bizarre mental images. *Journal of Experimental Psychology: Learning, Memory, and Cognition, 8*, 148–152.

Ong, W. J. (2002). *Orality and literacy: The technologizing of the word* (2nd ed.). Routledge: New York.

Owensworth, L., & MacFarland, K. (1999). Memory remediation in long-term acquired brain injury: Two approaches in diary training. *Brain Injury, 13*, 605–626.

Packman, J. L., & Battig, W. F. (1978). Effects of different kinds of semantic processing on memory for words. *Memory and Cognition, 6*, 502–508.

Paivio, A. (1969). Mental imagery in associative learning and memory. *Psychological Review, 76*, 241–263.

Paivio, A. (1971). *Imagery and verbal processes.* New York: Holt, Rinehart, and Winston.

Paivio, A. (1991). Dual coding theory: Retrospect and current status. *Canadian Journal of Psychology, 45*, 255–287.

Paivio, A., & Desrochers, A. (1981). Mnemonic techniques in second language learning. *Journal of Educational Psychology, 73*, 780–795.

Parenté, R., & Herrmann, D. (2003). *Retraining cognition: Techniques and applications.* Austin, TX: PRO-ED.

Parenté, R., & Stapleton, M. (1993). An empowerment model of memory training. *Applied Cognitive Psychology, 7*, 585–602.

Park, D. C., Smith, A. D., & Cavanaugh, J. C. (1990). Metamemories of memory researchers. *Memory and Cognition, 18*, 321–327.

Pashler, H., Rohrer, D., Cepeda, N. J., & Carpenter, S. K. (2007). Enhancing learning and retarding forgetting: Choices and consequences. *Psychonomic Bulletin and Review, 14*, 187–193.

Patton, G. W. (1986). The effect of the *phonetic mnemonic* system on memory for numeric material. *Human Learning: Journal of Practical Research and Applications, 5*, 21–28.

Patton, G. W., D'Agaro, W. R., & Gaudette, M. D. (1991). The effect of subject-generated and experimenter-supplied code words on the phonetic mnemonic system. *Applied Cognitive Psychology, 5*, 135–148.

Patton, G. W., & Lanzy, P. D. (1987). Testing the limits of the phonetic mnemonic system. *Applied Cognitive Psychology, 1*, 263–271.

Peterson, L. R., & Peterson, M. J. (1959). Short-term retention of individual verbal items. *Journal of Experimental Psychology, 58*, 193–198.

Piaget, J. (1928). *Judgment and reasoning in the child.* New York: Harcourt Brace.

Pressley, M., Levin, J. R., & Miller, G. E. (1981). The keyword methods and children's learning of foreign words with abstract meanings. *Canadian Journal of Psychology, 35*, 283–287.

Pyc, M. A., & Rawson, K. A. (2009). Testing the retrieval effort hypothesis: Does greater difficulty correctly recalling information lead to higher levels of memory? *Journal of Memory and Language, 60*, 437–447.

Raugh, M. R., & Atkinson, R. C. (1975). A mnemonic method for learning a second-language vocabulary. *Journal of Educational Psychology, 67*, 1–16.

Rawson, K. A., & Van Overschelde, J. P. (2008). How does knowledge promote memory? The distinctiveness theory of skilled memory. *Journal of Memory and Language, 58*, 646-658.

Reason, J. T., & Lucas, D. (1984). Using cognitive diaries to investigate naturally occurring memory blocks. In J. E. Harris & P. E. Morris (Eds.), *Everyday memory errors, actions, and absentmindedness* (pp. 53–70). London: Academic Press.

Reddy, B. G., & Bellezza, F. S. (1986). Interference between mnemonic and categorical organization in memory. *Bulletin of the Psychonomic Society, 24*, 169–171.

Rees, L., Marshall, S., Hartridge, C., Mackie, D., & Weiser, M., for the ERABI Group. (2007). Cognitive interventions post acquired brain injury. *Brain Injury, 21*, 161–200.

Resnick, L. B. (1981). Instructional psychology. *Annual Review of Psychology, 32*, 659–704.

Richardson, J. T. E. (1978). Reported mediators and individual differences in mental imagery. *Memory and Cognition, 6*, 376–378.

Richardson, J. T. E. (1995). The efficacy of imagery mnemonics in memory remediation. *Neuropsychologia, 33*, 1345–1357.

Roediger, H. L. (1980). The effectiveness of four mnemonics in ordering recall. *Journal of Experimental Psychology: Human Learning and Memory, 6*, 558–567.

Roediger, H. L., & Karpicke, J. D. (2007). The power of testing memory: Basic research and implications for educational practice. *Perspectives on Psychological Science, 1*, 181–211.

Roediger, H. L., III, & McDermott, K. B. (1995). Creating false memories: Remembering words not presented in lists. *Journal of Experimental Psychology: Learning, Memory, and Cognition, 21*, 803–814.

Roediger, H. L., Stellon, C. C., & Tulving, E. (1977). Inhibition from part-list cues and rate of recall. *Journal of Experimental Psychology: Human Learning and Memory, 3*, 174–188.

Rogers, T. B., Kuiper, N. A., & Kirker, W. S. (1977). Self reference and the encoding of personal information. *Journal of Personality and Social Psychology, 35*, 677–688.

Rohling, M. L., Faust, M. E., Beverly, B., & Demakis, G. (2009). Effectiveness of cognitive rehabilitation following acquired brain injury: A meta-analytic re-examination of Cicerone et al.'s (2000, 2005) systematic reviews. *Neuropsychology, 23*, 20–39.

Rönnlund, M., Nyberberg, L., Bäckman, L., & Nilsson, L. G. (2005). Stability, growth, and decline in adult life span development of declarative memory: Cross-sectional and longitudinal data from a population-based study. *Psychology and Aging, 20*, 3–18.

Rosenheck, M. B., Levin, M. E., & Levin, J. R. (1989). Learning botany concepts mnemonically: Seeing the forest and the trees. *Journal of Educational Psychology, 81*(2), 196–203.

Rubin, D. C. (1995). *Memory in oral traditions: The cognitive psychology of epic, ballads, and counting-out rhymes.* New York: Oxford University Press.

Rubin, D. C., & Wallace, W. T. (1989). Rhyme and reason: Analyses of dual retrieval cues. *Journal of Experimental Psychology: Learning, Memory, and Cognition, 24*, 698–709.

Ryan, D., Blakeslee, T., & Furst, D. (1986). Mental practice and motor skill learning: An indirect test of the neuromuscular feedback hypothesis. *International Journal of Sport Psychology, 17*, 60–70.

Schacter, D., & Tulving, E. (1994). What are the memory systems of 1994? In D. Schacter & E. Tulving (Eds.), *Memory systems.* Cambridge, MA: MIT Press.

Schacter, D. L., Wagner, A. D., & Buckner, R. L. (2000). Memory systems of 1999. In E. Tulving & F. I. M. Craik (Eds.), *The Oxford handbook of memory.* New York: Oxford University Press.

Schacter, D. S., & Wiseman, A. L. (2006). Reducing memory errors: The distinctiveness heuristic. In R. R. Hunt & J. B. Worthen (Eds.), *Distinctiveness and memory* (pp. 89–107). New York: Oxford University Press.

Schultz, D. P., & Schultz, S. E. (1992). *A history of modern psychology* (5th ed.). Orlando, FL: Harcourt Brace.

Sellen, A. J. (1994). Detection of everyday errors. *Applied Psychology: An International Review, 43*, 475–498.

Slamecka, N. J. (1985). Ebbinghaus: Some associations. *Journal of Experimental Psychology: Learning, Memory, and Cognition, 11*, 414–435.

Slamecka, N. J., & Graf, P. (1978). The generation effect: Delineation of a phenomenon. *Journal of Experimental Psychology: Human Learning and Memory, 4*, 592–604.

Sohlberg, M. M. (2005). External aids for management of memory impairment. In W. M. High, A. M. Sander, M. A. Struchen, & K. A. Hart (Eds.), *Rehabilitation for traumatic brain injury* (pp. 41–71). New York: Oxford University Press.

Soler, M. J., & Ruiz, J. C. (1996). The spontaneous use of memory aids at different educational levels. *Applied Cognitive Psychology, 10*, 41–51.

Solso, R. L., & Biersdorff, K. K. (1975). *Recall* under conditions of cumulative cues. *Journal of General Psychology, 93*, 233–246.

Stalder, D. R. (2005). Learning and motivational benefits of acronym use in introductory psychology. *Teaching of Psychology, 32,* 222–228.

Stallings, S. L., & Derry, S. J. (1986). Can an *advance organizer* technique compensate for poor reading conditions? *Journal of Experimental Education, 54,* 217–222.

Sweeney, C. A., & Bellezza, F. S. (1982). Use of keyword mnemonics in learning English vocabulary. *Human Learning, 1,* 155–163.

Tanner, W. P., & Swets, J. A. (1954). A decision-making theory of visual detection. *Psychological Review, 61,* 401–409.

Thomas, M. H., & Wang, A. Y. (1996). Learning by the keyword mnemonic: Looking for long-term benefits. *Journal of Experimental Psychology: Applied, 2,* 330-342.

Thompson, C. P., Cowan, T. M., & Frieman, J. (1993). *Memory search by a memorist.* Hillsdale, NJ: Lawrence Erlbaum.

Thompson, D. N. (1998). Using *advance organizers* to facilitate reading comprehension among older adults. *Educational Gerontology, 24,* 625–638.

Thomson, D. L., & Tulving, E. (1970). Associative encoding and retrieval: Weak and strong cues. *Journal of Experimental Psychology, 86,* 255–262.

Thorndike, E. L. (1907). *The elements of psychology* (2nd ed.). New York: A. G. Seiler.

Thorndike, E. L. (1911). *Animal intelligence.* New York: Macmillan.

Thurman, D. J., Alverson, C., Dunn, K. A., Guerrero, J., & Sniezek, J. E. (1999). Traumatic brain injury in the United States: A public health perspective. *Journal of Head Trauma Rehabilitation, 14,* 602–615.

Tinti, C., Cornoldi, C., & Marschark, M. (1997). Modality-specific auditory imaging and the interactive imagery effect. *European Journal of Cognitive Psychology, 9,* 417–436.

Toth, J. P., Daniels, K. A., & Jacoby, L. L. (2005). *Art Dealer: A computer game for enhancing cognition in older adults.* Unpublished manuscript, available from Jeffrey P. Toth, tothj@uncw.edu.

Troutt-Ervin, E. D. (1990). Application of keyword mnemonics to learning terminology in the college classroom. *Journal of Experimental Education, 59,* 31–41.

Tulving, E. (1962). Subjective organization in free recall of "unrelated" words. *Psychological Review, 69,* 344–354.

Tulving, E. (1972). Episodic and semantic memory. In E. Tulving & W. Donaldson (Eds.), *Organization of memory.* New York: Academic Press.

Tulving, E. (1983). *Elements of episodic memory.* Oxford, UK: Oxford University Press.

Tulving, E. (1985). How many memory systems are there? *American Psychologist, 40,* 385–398.

Tulving, E., & Pearlstone, Z. (1966). Availability versus accessibility of information in memory for words. *Journal of Verbal Learning and Verbal Behavior, 5,* 381–391.

Tulving, E., & Thomson, D. M. (1973). Encoding specificity and retrieval processes in episodic memory. *Psychological Review, 80,* 352-373.

Van Dam, G., Brinkerink-Carlier, M., & Kok, I. (1985). The influence of embellishment and prequestions on free recall of a text. *Journal of General Psychology, 112,* 211–219.

Van Den Broek, M. D., Downes, J., Johnson, Z., et al. (2000). Evaluation of an electronic memory aid in the neuropsychological rehabilitation of prospective memory deficits. *Brain Injury, 14,* 455–462.

Van Hell, J. G., & Mahn, A. C. (1997). Keyword mnemonics versus rote rehearsal: Learning concrete and abstract foreign words by experienced and inexperienced learners. *Language Learning, 47,* 507–546.

Van Overschelde, J. P., Rawson, K. A., Dunlosky, J., & Hunt, R. R. (2005). Distinctive processing underlies skilled memory. *Psychological Science, 16*, 358–361.

Veit, D. T., Scruggs, T. E., & Mastropieri, M. A. (1986). Extended mnemonic instruction with learning disabled students. *Journal of Educational Psychology, 78*, 300–308.

Verhaeghen, P., Marcoen, A., & Goossens, L. (1992). Improving memory performance in the aged through mnemonic training: A meta-analytic study. *Psychology and Aging, 7*, 242–251.

Viertel, P. (1953). *White hunter, black heart*. New York: Doubleday.

Waddill, P. J., & McDaniel, M. A. (1998). Distinctiveness effects in recall: Differential processing or privileged retrieval? *Memory and Cognition, 26*, 108–120.

Wade, D. T. (2005). Applying the WHO ICF framework to the rehabilitation of patients with cognitive deficits. In P. W. Halligan & D. T. Wade (Eds.), *The effectiveness of rehabilitation for cognitive deficits* (pp. 31–42). Oxford, UK: Oxford University Press.

Waite, C. J., Blick, K. A., & Boltwood, C. E. (1971). Prior usage to the first-letter technique. *Psychological Reports, 29*, 630.

Wallace, W. T. (1994). Memory for music: effect of melody on recall of text. *Journal of Experimental Psychology: Learning, Memory, and Cognition, 20*, 1471-1485.

Wallace, W. T., & Rubin, D. C. (1988). Memory of a ballad singer. In M. M. Gruneberg, P. E. Morris, & R. N. Sykes (Eds.), *Practical aspects of memory: Current research and issues, Vol. 1: Memory in everyday life* (pp. 257–262). Oxford, UK: Wiley & Sons.

Wallace, W. T., & Rubin, D. C. (1991). Characteristics and constraints in ballads and their effects on memory. *Discourse Processes, 14*, 181–202.

Wang, A. Y. (1983). Individual differences in learning speed. *Journal of Experimental Psychology: Learning, Memory, and Cognition, 9*, 300–311.

Wang, A. Y., & Thomas, M. H. (1992). The effect of imagery-based mnemonics on long-term retention of Chinese characters. *Language Learning, 42*, 359–376.

Wang, A. Y., & Thomas, M. H. (1995). The effect of keywords on long-term retention: Help or hindrance? *Journal of Educational Psychology, 87*, 468–475.

Wang, A. Y., & Thomas, M. H. (2000). Looking for long-term effects on serial recall: The legacy of Simonides. *American Journal of Psychology, 113*, 331–340.

Wang, A. Y., Thomas, M. H., Inzana, C. M., & Primicerio, L. J. (1993). Long-term retention under conditions of intentional learning and the keyword mnemonic. *Bulletin of the Psychonomic Society, 31*, 545–547.

Wang, A. Y., Thomas, M. H., & Ouellette, J. A. (1992). Keyword mnemonic and retention of second-language vocabulary words. *Journal of Educational Psychology, 84*, 520–528.

Watson, J. B. (1914). *Behavior: An introduction to comparative psychology*. New York: Holt.

White, K. D., Ashton, R., & Lewis, S. (1979). Learning a complex skill: Effects of mental practice, physical practice, and imagery ability. *International Journal of Sport Psychology, 10*, 71-78.

Wilding, J., & Valentine, E. (1985). One man's memory for prose, faces, and names. *British Journal of Psychology, 76*, 215–219.

Wilding, J., & Valentine, E. (1991). Superior memory ability. In J. Weinman & J. Hunter (Eds.), *Memory: Neurochemical and abnormal perspectives* (pp. 209–228). New York: Harwood.

Wilding, J., & Valentine, E. (1994). Memory champions. *British Journal of Psychology, 85*, 231–244.

Wilding, J., & Valentine, E. (1997). *Superior memory*. Hove, England: Psychology Press.

Wilding, J. M., & Valentine, E. R. (2006). Exceptional memory. In K. S. Ericsson, N. Charness, P. J. Feltovich, & R. R. Hoffman (Eds.), *The Cambridge handbook of expertise and expert performance*. New York: Cambridge University Press.

Wilson, B. A. (1995). Management and remediation of memory problems in brain-injured adults. In A. D. Baddeley, B. A. Wilson, & F. N. Watts (Eds.), *Handbook of memory disorders* (pp. 451–479). Chichester, England: Wiley.

Wilson, B. A. (2005). Management and remediation of memory problems in brain-injured adults. In A. Baddeley, M. Kopelman, & B. Wilson (Eds.), *The essential handbook of memory disorders for clinicians*. West Sussex, England: John Wiley.

Wilson, B. A. (2007). Cognitive rehabilitation. In F. Durso (Ed.), *Handbook of applied cognition* (2nd ed., pp. 585–604). West Sussex, England: John Wiley.

Wilson, B. A., Baddeley, A., Evans, J., & Shiel, A. (1994). Errorless learning in rehabilitation of memory impaired people. *Neuropsychological Rehabilitation, 4*, 307–326.

Wilson, B. A., Baddeley, A. D., & Kapur, N. (1995). Dense amnesia in a professional musician following Herbes simplex virus encephalitis. *Journal of Clinical and Experimental Psychology, 17*, 668–681.

Wilson, B. A., Emslie, H. C., Quirk, K., & Evans, J. (2001). Reducing everyday memory and planning problems by means of a paging system: A randomized crossover study. *Journal of Neurology, Neurosurgery, and Psychiatry, 70*, 477–482.

Wilson, B. A., Herbert, C. M., & Shiel, A. (2003). *Behavioral approaches in neuropsychological rehabilitation: Optimizing rehabilitation procedures*. Hove, England: Psychology Press.

Wilson, B. A., J. C., & Hughes, E. (1997). Coping with amnesia: The natural history of a compensatory memory system. In A. J. Parkin (Ed.), *Case studies in the neuropsychology of memory* (pp. 179–190). Hove, England: Psychology Press/Lawrence Erlbaum.

Winnick, W. A., & Brody, N. (1984). Auditory and visual imagery in free recall. *Journal of Psychology, 118*, 17–29.

Wollen, K. A., & Cox, S. (1981). Sentence cuing and the effectiveness of bizarre imagery. *Journal of Experimental Psychology: Human Learning and Memory, 7*, 386–392.

Wollen, K. A., & Margres, M. G. (1987). Bizarreness and the imagery multiprocess model. In M. A. McDaniel & M. Pressley (Eds.), *Imagery and related mnemonic processes: Theories, individual differences and applications* (pp. 103–127). New York: Springer-Verlag.

Wong, M. R. (1974). Additive effects of *advance organizers*. *Journal of Structural Learning, 4*, 165–173.

Wood, L. E., & Pratt, J. D. (1987). Pegword mnemonic as an aid to memory in the elderly: A comparison of four age groups. *Educational Gerontology, 13*, 325–339.

World Health Organization. (2001). *The international classification of functioning, disability, and health (ICF)*. Geneva: Author.

Worthen, J. B. (2006). Resolution of discrepant memory strengths: An explanation of the effects of bizarreness on memory. In R. R. Hunt & J. B. Worthen (Eds.), *Distinctiveness and memory* (pp. 133–156). New York: Oxford University Press.

Worthen, J. B., Fontenelle, S. F., Deschamps, J. D., & Foreman, E. (2008, November). *Limitations of second-language instruction using the keyword method.* Paper presented at the 48th annual meeting of the Psychonomic Society, Chicago.

Worthen, J. B., Garcia-Rivas, G., Green, C. R., & Vidos, R. A. (2000). Tests of a cognitive resource allocation account of the bizarreness effect. *Journal of General Psychology, 127,* 117–144.

Worthen, J. B., & Hunt, R. R. (2008). Mnemonics: Underlying processes and practical applications. In H. L. Roediger, III (Ed.), *Cognitive psychology of memory.* Vol. 2 of *Learning and memory: A comprehensive reference,* 4 vols. (J. Byrne, Ed.). Oxford, UK: Elsevier.

Worthen, J. B., & Loveland, J. M. (2003). Disruptive effects of bizarreness in free and cued recall of self-performed and other-performed acts: The costs of item-specific processing. In S. P. Shohov (Ed.), *Advances in psychology research* (Vol. 24, pp. 3–17). Hauppauge, NY: Nova Science.

Wynn, T., & Coolidge, F. L. (2003). The role of working memory in the evolution of managed foraging. *Before Farming, 2,* 1–16.

Wynn, T., & Coolidge, F. L. (2008). A stone-age meeting of minds. *American Scientist, 96,* 44–51.

Yarmey, A. D. (1984). Bizarreness effects in mental imagery. In A. A. Sheikh (Ed.), *International review of mental imagery* (Vol. 1, pp. 57–76). New York: Human Sciences Press.

Yates, F. A. (1966). *The art of memory.* London: Routledge & Kegan Paul.

Yeo, R. (2004). John Locke's "new method" of commonplacing: Managing memory and information. *Eighteenth-Century Thought, 2,* 1–38.

Yoshimura, E. K., Moely, B. E., & Shapiro, S. I. (1971). The influence of age and presentation order upon children's free recall and learning to learn. *Psychonomic Science, 23,* 261–263.

Young, R. K. (1985) Ebbinghaus: Some consequences. *Journal of Experimental Psychology: Learning, Memory, and Cognition, 11,* 491–495.

Ziegler, S. G. (1987). Comparison of imagery styles and past experience in skill performance. *Perceptual and Motor Skills, 64,* 579–586.

Zoller, C. L., Workman, J. S., & Kroll, N. E. A. (1989). The bizarre mnemonic: The effect of retention interval and mode of presentation. *Bulletin of the Psychonomic Society, 27,* 215–218.

AUTHOR INDEX

SUBJECT INDEX

A

Absentminded forgetting, 22
Acronym mnemonics, 69–72, 72t
Adjectives, free recall and, 45
Advance organizers, overview of, 78–79
Age, confounding and, 117
Aging, 107, 118–120, 126
Aitken, Alexander, 85–88, 91
Alarms, 31, 127
Alzheimer's disease, 107, 109
Amnesia, 112–113
Angiosperms example, 98–99, 99f
Antiquities Act example, 60–62
Aptitude, memory and, 27–28
Armed Services Vocational Aptitude
    Battery, 27
ARrOW acronym, 72t
Art Dealer, 119–120
Artists example, 100–101
Associationists, 8
Associations, semantic memory and, 21
Attention, encoding and, 38
Auditory mental imagery, overview of,
    51–52
Automatic processes, 112, 119
Avoiding-repetitions procedure, 119
Awareness, 21

B

Bacon, Francis, 6
BEDMAS acronym, 72t
Behaviorism, 11
Bias, 25–26
Binoculars example, 66
Birding example, 66
Bizarre imagery
    acceptance of, 12
    Bacon and, 6
    method of loci and, 58
    Middle Ages and, 3–4, 5
    personality differences and, 28
    visual mental imagery and, 50
Bradwardine, Thomas, 5
Brain injuries, 107
BRASS acronym, 72t
Brown-Peterson test of short-term memory, 89
Bruno, Giordano, 6

C

CATARAct acronym, 72t
Catchpenny criticism, 10
Categorical mnemonics, overview of, 76–77
Cerebral hemorrhage, 113
Chaco Canyon, 60–62
Cicero, Marcus Tullius, 3
Cognition, 37–44
Cognitive development, theory of, 70–71
Cognitive loads, phonetic system and, 67
Cognitive rehabilitation
    evaluating effectiveness of use in,
        115–117
    goals of, 108–109
    healthy aging and, 118–120
    issues for research in, 117–118
    mnemonology in, 126–127
    overview of use in, 107–108, 151
    techniques for use in, 109–115, 114f
Commonplace book method, 7
Compensatory training, 126–127
Complexity, costs and, 105
Comprehension, 106
Computer games, 119–120
Concealed mental images, 56
Conditioning, 128
Confounding, research and, 117
Conscious awareness, 21
Conservationist example, 56–58
Conservative response bias, 25
Conservativism, bizarre imagery and, 28
Context, memory and, 20
Control groups, research and, 117
Controlled processes, 112, 119
Coral snake example, 74
Costs of mnemonic use, 104–105
Cranial nerves example, 71
Cue diagnosticity, 43
Cued recall, 23–26, 43–44, 62–65, 73
Cues, 43, 49, 71–72

D

DABDA acronym, 70
D-CUP acronym, 72t
Devils Tower, 60–62
Dicson, Alexander, 6